TAX ANSWERS AT A GLANCE

Ashley Smith FCCA CTA ATT
Iain Watson

Tax Answers at a Glance
by Ashley Smith and Iain Watson

1st edition 2001
2nd edition 2002
3rd edition 2003
4th edition 2004
5th edition 2005
6th edition 2006
7th edition 2007
8th edition 2008
9th edition 2009
10th edition 2010
11th edition 2010
12th edition 2011
13th edition 2012
14th edition 2013
15th edition 2014
16th edition 2015
17th edition 2016

ISBN: 9781910143339

Ebook ISBN: 9781910143346

Exclusion of Liability and Disclaimer

Contents

'In this world nothing can be said to be certain, except death and taxes.'

Benjamin Franklin

About the authors

Ashley Smith FCCA CTA ATT is the proprietor of H M Williams Chartered Certified Accountants.

Iain Watson is Tax Manager at H M Williams; formerly with HM Revenue & Customs, he offers an invaluable insider's view of tax legislation.

Representing H M Williams, the authors have been winners of the prestigious Butterworth Tolley Best Tax Team Award. The firm has also been awarded the coveted *Daily Telegraph*/Energis Customer Service Award in the Professional and Business Services, Small Organisation category. In 2007, it won the 2020 award for the most innovative medium-sized UK accountancy practice.

Important facts

Welcome to *Tax Answers at a Glance*. It's packed with information and advice on your obligations and rights as a taxpayer.

The information this book contains has been carefully compiled from professional sources, but its accuracy is not guaranteed, as laws and regulations may change in the Budget and be subject to changing interpretations. Please be aware that the details referred to in this book have been announced by the Chancellor of the Exchequer in various recent Budgets.

Tax regulations are stated as at 6 April 2016.

Neither this nor any other publication can take the place of an accountant on important tax matters. Common sense should determine whether you need the assistance of an accountant rather than relying solely on the information in *Tax Answers at a Glance*.

Introduction

There are many books on tax, for both the professional and lay reader, but our impression is that most of them seem to look rather heavy, even if they are not. As a practising accountants we know only too well how clients will phone in with questions (perhaps quite simple questions) and all they want is a simple answer. If our clients are asking such questions, then there must be a lot of taxpayers who don't use the services of a professional accountant and who have similar questions that they would like answered.

Accordingly, this book is written almost in the style of a catechism. It's meant to home in on the questions, giving answers at a glance, rather than giving all the background information which, to be realistic, most taxpayers don't want or need.

Our aim is for this book to be published on an annual basis and so, with these regular updates, there are bound to be more questions that readers would like us to answer than we have included in this latest edition. We would welcome contributions from our readership because their feedback will enable the next edition to be a further improvement on what we hope is already a sensible way of providing *Tax Answers at a Glance*. If you have any comments or questions, please call us on 01752 334 950.

CHAPTER 1
Tax in general

What are the different taxes that we have to pay?

Between us (private individuals and businesses, etc.), we pay the following taxes:

- Income Tax
- National Insurance contributions
- Value Added Tax
- Capital Gains Tax
- Inheritance Tax
- Stamp Duty
- Stamp Duty Land Tax
- Corporation Tax
- Petroleum Revenue Tax
- Fuel Duty
- Tobacco Products Duty
- Spirits Duty
- Wine and Made-Wine Duty
- Beer Duty
- Cider Duty

- Machine Games Duty
- Gaming Duty
- General Betting Duty
- Pool Betting Duty
- Bingo Duty
- Remote Gaming Duty
- Lottery Duty
- Air Passenger Duty
- Insurance Premium Tax
- Landfill Tax
- Aggregates Levy
- Climate Change Levy
- Bank Levy
- Bank Surcharge
- Horserace Betting Levy
- Customs Duty
- Excise Duty
- Vehicle Excise Duty
- Business Rates
- Council Tax
- Annual Tax on Enveloped Dwellings

It's quite a list, isn't it? A summary of the actual tax rates and allowances is provided at Appendix 1.

How much does the government raise in tax and what does it spend it on?

The government expects to have raised, approximately, the following in tax in 2016/17:

	2015/16 £bn	2016/17 £bn	Selected percentages	Estimated av. paid by each adult annually
Income Tax	170	182	25	£3,714
Corporation Tax (net)	44	44	6	
Petroleum Revenue Tax	-1	-1		
Capital Gains Tax	7	7	1	
Inheritance Tax	5	5		
Stamp Duty	3	3		
Stamp Duty Land Tax	11	13		
Value Added Tax & Refunds	130	135	19	2,612
Fuel Duties	28	28	4	£571
Tobacco Duties	9	9		
Spirit Duties	3	3		
Wine Duties	4	4		
Beer & Cider Duties	4	4		
Air Passenger Duty	3	3		
Insurance Premium Tax	4	5		
National Insurance	115	127	18	£2,591
Climate Change levy	2	2		
Other HMRC receipts	7	7		
Vehicle Excise Duties	6	6	1	£122
Bank Levy & Surcharge	4	4		
Business Rates	28	28	4	
Council Tax	29	30	4	£1,037
Other Taxes & Receipts	18	20		
	633	**668**		
Government Interest & Surpluses	51	51		
Overall Total income	**684**	**719**		

Of the £182bn raised in Income Tax, £152bn is from PAYE and £30bn from Self Assessment.

If we assume a UK population of 65 million people, the above income figure represents £11,031 for every man, woman and child in the country per year, or £30.22 per day.

On the table above we have seen that in 2016/17 the government intends to raise £717 billion. The government intends to spend £772 billion roughly as follows:

	2015/16 £bn	2016/17 £bn
Health	141	145
Social Security and Social Services	292	270
Public order and safety	34	34
Defence	45	46
Education	99	102
Interest	35	39
Housing	28	34
Transport	29	29
Industry, agriculture and employment	24	24
Others, including EU transactions	46	49
Total	**773**	**772**

Based on these figures there will be a deficit in 2016/17 of about £55 billion.

When are the tax rates changed?

Recent governments have changed the method of deciding when tax rates should be changed (in other words, they have hopped about a bit), but, in principle, the announcements of the tax rates are given either in the Autumn Statement in December or in the Budget Statement in March. Those rates and allowances usually come into force on 6 April immediately following.

When it comes to National Insurance, these changes are also announced in the autumn. This gives HM Revenue & Customs (HMRC) and employers the chance to be prepared for the changes some months later.

The Chancellor has sometimes announced changes to other taxes for future years (i.e. beyond the immediately succeeding year) in his Budget in March and so, to a certain extent, tax advisers have known a few tax rates for a considerable period in advance.

What is the Income Tax year?

The Income Tax year runs from 6 April in one year to 5 April in the next. One of the former contributing authors of this book spent a considerable amount of time badgering HMRC, Chancellors and Treasury officials to change this cumbersome system by using a more sensible date. Corporation Tax ends its financial years on 31 March and it would make sense for the government to move the Income Tax year by a few days so that both tax year ends are coterminous. The reason the tax year ends on 5 April is not a logical one but this is an explanation of how it came about:

In the old days, and we are talking hundreds of years ago, the Income Tax year began on 25 March (the Feast of the Annunciation or Lady Day). Up to 1752 there were two European calendars and they had drifted apart by a few days. Britain used the Julian Calendar, devised at the time of Julius Caesar, while the rest of the Continent (pretty well all the rest) used the Gregorian Calendar (introduced by Pope Gregory the Great), which meant that by the time we had reached 1752, the Continent was 11 days ahead of us. In that year the two calendars merged and Britain 'lost' 11 days. The Treasury said that it could not afford to lose 11 days and added 11 days on to the end of the Income Tax year. This meant that the Income Tax year in 1753 ended on 4 April.

In 1800, our Treasury, for some reason, thought that there was a leap year. The formula for leap years is that they are years which can be divided by four and, when there is a centenary year, when they can be divided by 400. 1800 could not be divided by 400 to give a whole number result and so it was not a leap year – our Treasury thought otherwise. So the Treasury added an extra day to the Income Tax year at that stage resulting in a tax year end of 5 April.

What are Business Rates and Council Tax, and how is that money spent?

Business Rates are the rates paid by businesses to central government via their local councils. They are like a tax, but they don't go towards local services, except as part of the government's handout to local authorities. They are assessed on the area of space occupied by businesses.

Council Tax is collected by local councils and goes towards the following local services:

*   Planning and economic development

*   Recreation and tourism

*   Environmental health

*   Refuse collection

*   Education

*   Social Services

*   Police

*   Fire

Council Tax in England and Scotland (Rates in Northern Ireland) is assessed on the market value of domestic properties as at 1 April 1991. In Wales, the valuation date was 1 April 2003. Properties are then graded in bands A to H. There is a 25 per cent discount where only one person lives in a property. There can be a 100 per cent Council Tax surcharge if a property has been empty for more than a year. Some councils charge extra Council Tax for second homes.

What is HM Revenue & Customs and what is HM Treasury?

HM Revenue & Customs (HMRC) is the government department that is responsible for collecting most of the nation's taxes. HMRC advises the

Treasury on tax matters generally, but it's the Treasury, controlled by the government in power at the time, that decides how much tax it wants to raise from taxpayers. It then works with HMRC to devise a system that enables that money to be collected.

Within HMRC, there are Inspectors of Taxes, who check that the correct amount of tax is being paid by individuals, trusts and companies. There are also debt recovery people, who make sure that the tax is paid.

Tax and civil partners

All the tax legislation that applies to married couples has also applies to civil partners. For instance, civil partners are able to transfer assets to each other without incurring any Capital Gains Tax. However, if they have two main residences, they can only have one Principal Private Residence exemption, so they may wish to consider making an election to nominate the main residence. They are also able to transfer assets to each other free of Inheritance Tax.

Throughout this book any reference to married couples includes civil partners.

What tax do I pay when I buy a motor car?

New cars attract VAT at the standard rate.

You can only claim VAT back on the purchase of a car if:

- you are registered for VAT; and

- the vehicle is to be used exclusively for business purposes. This condition is virtually impossible to prove. The only people who can normally satisfy this condition are taxi drivers and driving instructors, and motor dealers who are buying the car as a stock item; or

- the vehicle is built to carry 12 or more seated persons and is to be used for business purposes.

Filling up the car is a pricey business. Look at how much of what you pay on the forecourt goes to the government:

	£	Government	Fuel companies	Garage proprietor
Government	0.58	0.58		
Fuel production and distribution	0.2		0.2	
Garage proprietor	0.05			0.05
Subtotal	0.83			
Add VAT	0.17	0.17		
Total per litre	**1.0**	**0.75**	**0.2**	**0.05**
	100%	**75%**	**20%**	**5%**

In other words, when you fill up with £60 of petrol:

£45.00 goes to the government

£12.00 goes to the fuel companies

£3.00 goes to the forecourt proprietor

So if you want to save tax, stop driving your car!

What tax do I pay when I buy fuel?

Let's say you have just paid £60 at the petrol station for fuel and used your credit card. How much of that amount goes to the government, how much to the garage, and how much to the fuel company?

The answer is pretty staggering: £45 goes to the government. Percentages vary depending on where you buy your fuel, but if you are paying £1.00 per litre, for example, the table opposite shows where your money goes.

What tax do I pay on celebratory fizz?

While the French pay only 6p duty per bottle of sparkling wine, in the UK we pay an enormous £2.97 per bottle. Analysis of a bottle of sparkling wine at the price of £7.99 shows that Excise Duty and VAT account for £3.81 of the total retail cost (48 per cent).

First introduced by Lord Goschen in the reign of Queen Victoria as a luxury levy to raise funds for the navy, many would argue that this tax is now outdated and should be brought in line with the duty on still wine, which stands at £1.94 per bottle (compared with 3p per bottle in France).

The Wine and Spirit Trade Association (WSTA) says that only around one in five bottles of sparkling wine sold in the UK is Champagne and that the overwhelming majority is wine such as Prosecco and Cava, which are priced to compete with still wine. In that sense, says the WSTA, the policy is an anachronism and there is no reason sparkling wine should be taxed any differently.

CHAPTER 2

Income Tax

What is Income Tax and what do we pay it on?

It may sound strange, but Income Tax is actually a temporary annual tax that the government decides to keep going by means of an annual Finance Bill. It was introduced in 1799 as a means of financing the Napoleonic Wars, but even though those wars are well past, Income Tax still seems to be with us.

Income Tax used to be divided into schedules, but it now comes under headings and these are:

- Trade profits (including all business profits)
- Property income
- Savings and investment income
- Employment income
- Pension income
- Mineral royalties
- Miscellaneous income (covers income not falling under the other headings)
- Earnings and pension income (which includes taxable Social Security benefits)

It might be more relevant if we now look at what income is not taxed (i.e. what is exempt):

- Adoption Allowances
- Annuities from gallantry awards
- Attendance Allowance
- Bereavement Payment
- Betting, lottery and pools winnings, and raffle prizes
- Car parking benefits
- Child Benefit
- Child dependency additions
- Child Tax Credit
- Child Trust Funds
- Children's savings accounts ('Junior ISAs')
- Christmas bonuses paid by the state to pensioners
- Compensation for loss of employment of up to £30,000 (professional advice must be sought)
- Compensation for mis-sold personal pensions
- Compensation paid to Equitable Life policyholders
- Council Tax Benefit
- Damages and compensation for personal injury, including interest
- Disability Living Allowance
- Educational Maintenance Allowance
- Electricity microgeneration for home use
- Foster Care Income
- Gifts for employees from third parties if they are under £250 a year
- Gratuities and bounties from the armed forces
- Guardian's Allowance
- Home improvement, repair and insulation grants
- Housing Benefit
- Incapacity Benefit (short-term – lower rate) for first 28 weeks
- Income Support
- Individual Savings Accounts (ISAs)
- Industrial injury benefits
- Insurance bond withdrawals of up to five per cent per year (this can be complicated and professional advice should be sought)
- Insurance policy payments (mortgage payment protection, permanent health, etc.)
- Interest from National Savings Certificates

- Interest on overpaid tax
- Invalidity pensions
- Jobfinder's Grant
- Life assurance policy bonuses and profits
- Long-service awards of up to £50 for each year of service (for employees)
- Lump sums from an approved pension scheme
- Maintenance or alimony payments
- Maternity Allowance
- Miners' Coal Allowance
- National Savings Certificates' increase in value
- Pension credits
- Pensions from Austria or Germany to victims of Nazi persecution
- Premium Bond prizes
- Provident benefits paid by a trade union of up to £4,000 for lump-sum payments
- Purchased life annuities – capital element only
- Rent-a-room relief up to £7,500 a year
- Save As You Earn Schemes (SAYE) bonuses and interest
- Scholarship income and bursaries
- Severe Disablement Allowances
- Share option profits made under an SAYE option scheme – Capital Gains Tax may be payable
- Shares awarded under an approved Share Incentive Plan (professional advice must be sought)
- Social fund payments
- Statutory Redundancy Pay
- Strike and unemployment pay from a trade union
- Student Grants
- Suggestion scheme awards
- Training allowances for reserve forces
- Travel to work on a works bus
- TV licence payment
- Vaccine damage payment
- Venture Capital Trust dividends
- War Disablement Benefits
- War Widows' Pension
- Winter fuel payments
- Woodlands income
- Working Tax Credit

What are the changes for Scottish taxpayers?

From 6 April 2016, Scottish taxpayers will start to pay the Scottish rate of Income Tax and consequently some of your tax will go to the Scottish government. See the table below to show how much of your tax will go to the Scottish government if you are a Scottish taxpayer:

UK rate for England, Wales and Northern Ireland	Income band	UK rate paid in Scotland	Scottish rate	Total rate for Scottish taxpayers
Basic rate 20%	£11,001 - £43,000	10%	10%	20%
Higher rate 40%	£43,001 - £150,000	30%	10%	40%
Additional rate 45%	Over £150,000	35%	10%	45%

Generally speaking, you will be a Scottish taxpayer if your only or main home is in Scotland. You will be notified by HMRC if they believe that you should be paying Scottish tax. However, if you live in England, but travel across the border to work, you will not be a Scottish taxpayer.

At the time of writing there has been much debate in Scotland about whether the rates of tax and the tax rate bands should be kept the same as in the rest of the UK. Certain Scottish politicians want to change the figures so watch this space ...

What is an annual Tax Return?

This is a form (SA100) issued each year to about nine million taxpayers, the purpose of which is for them to list their taxable income, their tax relievable expenses and their chargeable capital gains and, if they wish to do it themselves, calculate the overall tax due and the dates by which it should be paid. It can be completed manually or it can be submitted online.

Some taxpayers (mostly employees and pensioners) are now being issued with a shorter, simpler Short Tax Return (SA200). The taxpayer won't need to calculate his own liability, even if the Tax Return is submitted to HM Revenue & Customs (HMRC) after 30 September.

Paper Tax Returns must be filed by 31 October. Returns filed online must reach the Tax Office by 31 January. Failure to submit a Return on time may result in one or more penalties.

What is Simple Assessment?

In the 2015 Autumn Statement, it was announced that in the 2016/17 tax year HMRC would introduce a simpler system for paying tax. This will be aimed at taxpayers who are within self-assessment, but have 'simple' affairs. One does wonder why, if their affairs are that simple, they are within self-assessment! In any event, a taxpayer within self-assessment has to complete a Tax Return; and only when this is submitted to HMRC can HMRC really know all about the taxpayers affairs in that year.

HMRC advise that where they hold all of the data that they need to calculate a taxpayer's liability, and where existing payment processes are not available taxpayers will be sent a tax calculation and a demand for payment.

This development is concerning, as in our day-to-day experience HMRC regularly issue tax calculations that do not take into consideration the entirety of a taxpayer's affairs. If you receive a tax calculation from HMRC that you are not expecting, please check it carefully – or ask an accountant to do this for you. We are concerned that HMRC might raise an incorrect calculation, which is not in accord with the taxpayer's Tax Return. We are also concerned that this might be an attempt by HMRC to issue tax demands sooner than is appropriate under the self-assessment rules. We applaud simplification, but not if it is at the detriment of the taxpayer!

How do I know if I have to fill out a Tax Return and how do I get hold of one?

Generally speaking, you will **have** to complete a Tax Return if you:

- are self-employed;
- are in partnership;
- are in receipt of net income from land and property of more than £2,500 (or less if the tax cannot be dealt with through the PAYE coding system);
- are a director;
- incur taxable capital gains;
- earn over £50,000 pa and have children for whom Child Benefit is received.

And very importantly, if you:

- are sent one (if HMRC issues a Tax Return or a Notice to complete a Tax Return, it **has** to be completed by the taxpayer).

If in any doubt, contact HMRC, advise them of your circumstances, and get them to confirm whether you should fill out a Tax Return.

If you need to get hold of a Tax Return, contact your local Tax Office and ask it to send you one, or download one from the HMRC website. A checklist of what to keep for your Tax Return is provided at Appendix 2. Plans have been announced to phase out the traditional Tax Return. It seems likely that it will be replaced by a requirement to make quarterly online submissions of your income and expenditure to HMRC instead.

How do I work out how much tax I have to pay and when to pay it?

If you have to complete a Tax Return, included in the package will be a tax calculation guide for you to follow. It's not within the scope of this book to guide you through it (HMRC's form does it pretty well for you), but the main thing to bear in mind is that if you get your Tax Return submitted by 31 October each year, HMRC will work out for you how much tax you have to pay and when you have to pay it.

In principle, you make two payments a year. On 31 January each year you will pay the balance of the previous year's tax still owing plus, if your liability for the year is in excess of £1,000, one half of the previous year's tax liability as a first payment on account for the following year.

On 31 July each year you will pay the second half of last year's tax liability as a second payment on account. On 31 January following, you will find yourself paying any balance of tax that is due plus another payment on account based on this year's total tax bill, and so on.

If this all sounds very confusing, don't worry, it is! The government introduced self-assessment in 1997 with the intention that tax recording and calculations should be so simple that anybody could do it. If you ask most professional accountants nowadays, they would say that the current tax rules are so complicated they would find it very difficult to work out your tax liability if they didn't have the services of a computer.

What self-assessment has done is remove a lot of the work that was previously done in Tax Offices and dump it either on the taxpayer's own desk or, if the taxpayer is prepared to pay for it, in the offices of professional accountants, who now do the work that the Inspectors of Taxes formerly did.

In other words, self-assessment doesn't mean a simple calculation. It means 'It's up to you, mate, and don't blame us if we, HMRC, have made it difficult!'

What if my tax payments are late?

An interest charge is (i) automatic on late paid Income Tax, Class 4 National Insurance contributions and Capital Gains Tax, and (ii) added to existing liabilities and treated as tax due and payable.

A surcharge applies to all amounts due in respect of the previous tax year on 31 January following the end of that tax year and not paid within 30 days. This is five per cent of the amount unpaid more than 30 days after the due date with a further five per cent of the amount unpaid more than five months after the 30 days. Another five per cent surcharge arises if the tax remains unpaid after eleven months after the 30 days. However, the taxpayer may appeal against a surcharge if he has a reasonable excuse for non-payment. HMRC has the power to take money directly from the bank account of anyone who owes tax of more than £1,000, and has the means to pay it, but refuses to do so. Following consultation, this will only be taken if a minimum aggregate credit of £5,000 exists. The taxpayer has 30 days in which to appeal against this action if he believes the figure is incorrect. This is a highly controversial step that some people feel very strongly about.

What if I fail to complete a Tax Return on time?

If you have been issued with either a Self-Assessment Tax Return to complete, or a Notice to file a Tax Return, there are two important deadlines. If you are submitting a paper Tax Return, this has to be filed with HMRC by 31 October following the end of the tax year. If you are filing an electronic return, the deadline is 31 January following the end of the tax year. If you fail to submit your Return by the appropriate deadline, even if by only one day, you will receive a £100 penalty. This is regardless of whether or not you owe any tax.

Once the Return is three months late, daily penalties of £10 are charged up to a maximum of £900.

Once the Return is six months late, a charge of either five per cent of the tax due or £300, whichever is the greater, is charged.

Once the Return is 12 months late, a further penalty of five per cent or £300 (whichever is the greater) is charged. However, in serious cases the penalty can be increased to 100 per cent of the tax due.

Please note however, that if you are issued with a Self-Assessment Tax Return at any other time of the year apart from the bulk issue in April, that Return will have its own submission deadline, which may extend beyond 31 October and 31 January. The Return will show the filing deadline which applies to it and the penalties mentioned above will still be enforced if this specific deadline is not adhered to.

What can I set against my taxable income?

There is no quick answer to this question because there is a whole range of deductions, allowances and reliefs that taxpayers can claim. In principle, most taxpayers are entitled to a personal allowance (of which there is a number of different types). Apart from that it all depends on your circumstances. The sorts of relief that we, as accountants, see our clients claiming and that we can claim on their behalf are as follows:

- Relief for losses in a business
- Relief for certain professional subscriptions and expenses
- Relief for personal pension contributions
- Relief for Gift Aid payments
- Relief for investments made under either the Venture Capital Trust, Enterprise Investment or Seed Enterprise Investment Schemes
- Blind Person's Allowance
- Relief for interest on money borrowed for certain purposes
- Business expenses
- Certain allowances against capital gains

We do advise you to read HMRC's guidance notes that come with your Tax Return carefully, to be sure that you are claiming all of your reliefs – it simply isn't possible to list them all in the space of a book that gives you quick and easy to comprehend answers. You should also be aware that there is now a cap on the reliefs you can claim. This is set at the higher of £50,000 or 25 per cent of an individual's income. Charitable reliefs and share loss reliefs relating to Enterprise Investment Scheme or Seed Enterprise Investment Scheme investments and overlap reliefs are exempt from this cap.

What is the difference between earned and unearned income?

About 40 years ago it was better to be in receipt of earned income than unearned income because unearned income attracted investment income surcharge and there was a special earned income relief. Nowadays it's better to be in receipt of unearned income because earned income (salaries, wages, benefits, etc.) is not only taxable but is also subject to National Insurance contributions.

The distinction between the two is not a key one nowadays, but one of the more obvious distinctions arises in the case of a director shareholder. If he is paid a salary, then both the company and the director must pay National Insurance Contributions on that salary. The payment of (say) an additional £1,000 as earnings may result in about 45 per cent of that figure (basic rate tax, employers' NI and employees' NI) going to the government. If that same person is paid a dividend of £1,000 out of taxed profits, no further tax will be due to the government although, in due course, there will be tax payable by the director when it comes to completing his personal Tax Return, if his total dividend income for the year exceeds £5,000.

What are the rates of Income Tax?

In 2016/17, Income Tax is payable at the following rates:

- 'The savings rate' – 0 per cent on the first £5,000 of savings income, depending upon how much your non-savings income is. If your total gross income is above £17,000, then the 0 per cent band will not apply.

- 'The basic rate' – 20 per cent of your taxable income, up to £32,000.

- 'The dividend rate' – 7.5 per cent on dividend income falling within the above basic rate band, but in excess of the £5,000 dividend tax allowance.

- 'The higher rate' – 40 per cent on the next £32,000 – £150,000 of taxable income, other than dividends.

- 'The higher dividend rate' – 32.5 per cent on dividend income falling in the higher rate band, but in excess of the £5,000 dividend tax allowance.

- 'The additional rate' – 45 per cent on taxable income, other than dividends, in excess of £150,000.

- 'The additional dividend rate' – 38.1 per cent on taxable income consisting of dividends in excess of £150,000 after the £5,000 dividend tax allowance.

What are the personal reliefs and allowances?

The rates of the various personal reliefs and allowances for 2016/17 are:

£	
Personal*	11,000
Blind person's	2,290

Age	
Married couple's (age 75 and over) and born before 6 April 1935	**8,355

* the personal allowance in 2016/17 is gradually withdrawn for income over £100,000 at a rate of £1 of allowance lost for every £2 over £100,000.
** tax relief is restricted to 10%.

The income limit for Married Couples Allowance is £27,700 and the full allowance of £8,355 is reduced by £1 for every £2 that total income exceeds this figure. The Married Couples Allowance cannot be reduced below £3,220. The savings rate of zero per cent applies to the first £5,000, provided that total gross income does not exceed £16,000.

From 6 April 2015, it is possible for spouses and civil partners who were born after 5 April 1935 to transfer some of their personal allowance to each other. Neither party can be liable to tax at more than the basic rate, and the transfer can only be of unused personal allowances up to a maximum of ten per cent of the full allowance, i.e. in 2016/17, £1,100.

What tax relief can I claim on my payments of interest?

Opportunities to claim tax relief on payments of interest on loans are limited and are now restricted to the following:

- buying a share in a partnership or contributing capital to a partnership if you are a partner;
- buying shares in a close company (see page 119) or lending capital to it;
- buying plant and machinery for use in a job or partnership.

The interest paid (and not the capital) is deducted from your total income in the year of payment.

Can I get tax relief on my mortgage interest?

If you live in the property yourself, the short answer is 'No'. But, if you mortgage your house in order to buy a rental property, the answer will be 'Yes' – you can set off the mortgage interest against your rental income. However, from 6 April 2017, there are limitations placed upon the amount of relief that can be claimed; see 'What are the tax rules for buy-to-let investors?' on page 94.

Is there a right time to get married for Income Tax purposes?

The Married Couple's Allowance is now only available to those couples where either the husband or wife was born before 6 April 1935.

However, if you get married and you or your spouse meet the age criteria, you can claim 1/12 of the allowance for each month of the tax year concerned, starting with the month of marriage. So there is no 'right time' to get married for Income Tax purposes.

What is the Marriage Allowance?

From 6 April 2015, it has been possible, in certain circumstances, for married couples and civil partners to transfer some of their personal allowance to the other spouse/partner:

In the 2015/16 tax year, the amount that can be transferred is £1,060.

In the 2016/17 tax year, the amount that can be transferred is £1,100.

These transferable amounts are fixed, you cannot transfer more or less than these amounts. In 2015/16, the transfer was worth £212 and in 2016/17 it will be worth £220 in monetary terms to the recipient.

You can only receive the Marriage Allowance if you are liable to tax at the basic rate. If you are liable at the higher or additional rates, the transfer is not permitted. If you or your partner were born before 6th April 1935 and are eligible for the Married Couples Allowance, this may be more beneficial than the Marriage Allowance.

In order to obtain the Marriage Allowance the transferor needs to either:

* complete the relevant sections of their Tax Return to inform HMRC they wish to transfer part of their personal allowance; or
* apply online to inform HMRC they wish to transfer some of their personal allowance; or
* phone HMRC and inform them.

Unfortunately, at the time of writing there is no provision for the claim to be made on the recipient's tax return.

What happens to someone's Income Tax affairs when they die?

When someone dies, they are entitled to their normal full year's worth of allowances. A Tax Return will need to be completed for the period of 6 April up to the date of death and the tax worked out accordingly.

Income arising after death is treated as the income of the estate and becomes the responsibility of the trustees or executors. When the estate is distributed, both the capital and the income that has arisen since the date of death will be distributed according to the Will to the various beneficiaries and tax will be deducted from any income that has been received at the appropriate rate.

If you, as a beneficiary, are in receipt of income that has been credited to a deceased person's estate, then you will receive that income net of basic rate tax, and while you may have to pay higher-rate tax on the income there is also a chance that you might be able to claim some back or there may be no adjustment one way or the other. You should be issued with Form R185 ('Estate income'), which shows both the net payment and the tax paid/tax credit.

What should one do about the income of children and Income Tax?

Children, from the moment they are born, are entitled to a personal allowance and if they are in receipt of net income they are almost certainly entitled to a repayment of tax. Accordingly, where children are in receipt of income that has not arisen on money received from a parent, and from which tax has been deducted, it's potentially refundable. Get a tax claim form from the Tax Office or download it from the HMRC website (note that it's called a Claim for Repayment of Tax Deducted from Savings and Investments (R40) and not a Tax Return, but it amounts to the same thing). When you have completed it and sent it in, HMRC will either send a cheque in favour of the child or make a refund of tax straight to that child's own bank or building society account. The parent can also receive the refund on the child's behalf.

What are the most sensible sorts of investment for children for tax purposes?

The simplest answer is that savings accounts with building societies or banks that are in the children's name will pay the children interest gross (i.e. without tax deducted). There are also Junior ISAs which are specifically aimed at children.

It's still quite permissible for children to hold shares in companies, even though the tax credits on the dividends are not refundable.

If the children don't have any investments and if the parents have surplus after-tax income of their own which they give to their children, this is usually tax free in the children's hands and, if the parents are particularly wealthy, is a very useful way of transferring income to them, so that the children can accumulate a sum that can then be invested. However, once the income from the source exceeds £100 p.a. it will be taxed in the hands of the parents. Where parents transfer their own shares to their children, if the children are under 18, the income arising on these shares will be regarded as belonging to the parents, so this doesn't save tax.

The Child Trust Fund was a tax-free savings scheme designed for children born between 1 September 2002 and 2 January 2011. The government contributed £250 when the child was born and a further £250 (£500 for lower-income families) at the age of seven. Parents, family and friends could contribute a further £1,200 annually. The child was entitled to the fund at the age of 18 and there were no restrictions on how he used the money.

Children born after 2 January 2011, who are therefore not eligible for a Child Trust Fund, can invest in a Junior ISA (JISA). There is no tax to pay on any interest or gains made by a JISA. The total amount which can be invested is £4,080 in the year ending 5 April 2017. When the child becomes 18, he can withdraw the investment for any purpose.

What are the rules for charitable giving and Income Tax?

- Gifts of money to charities attract tax relief under the Gift Aid scheme. The gift is treated as if it had been made after deduction of

Income Tax at the basic rate. So if you give £80 to a charity, it can get £20 tax back. As a basic rate taxpayer, the making of the gift serves to extend the basic rate band by the gross equivalent of the payment. If you are a higher-rate taxpayer, you can claim a further £20 (or £25 if your top rate of tax is 45 per cent) of tax relief in your Tax Return.

- You need to complete a Gift Aid declaration. If you turn to Appendix 4, you will see an example of this and how it works. However, remember this will only work if you have paid more tax than will be reclaimed by the charity. Otherwise, HMRC will send you a bill for the difference.

- There is a generous tax relief for gifts of certain investments and property to charity.

Do be aware, however, that if a non-taxpayer makes a Gift Aid contribution, then they will be creating a tax liability for themselves in the amount of the tax relief which the charity is reclaiming.

What is 'Payroll Giving'?

If their employer is registered under the Payroll Giving scheme, employees can arrange a regular deduction from their pre-tax pay to go to a nominated charity, church or charitable association.

Employers need to sign an administration contract with an authorised Payroll Giving Agency. They do make a small administration charge that is either deducted from the donation or can be paid separately by the employer (around four to five per cent).

How do I reclaim overpaid tax?

If you are likely always to pay too much tax (through receiving no gross income, i.e. all your income suffers tax at source), HMRC will spot this and send you a tax claim form, R40 ('Claim for repayment of tax deducted from savings and investments'). This will be returnable to a Tax Office that deals solely with tax repayments. This scenario is frequently encountered by the young and the elderly.

If, on the other hand, you normally pay tax but in a certain year discover that you have overpaid, tick the appropriate box on the Tax Return and you can claim for the money to be refunded to you. If you leave the overpayment un-refunded, it will go to reduce your future year's tax payments. Generally speaking, the repayment will be processed more quickly if paid directly into a bank/building society account rather than if paid by cheque.

What are the rules regarding pre-owned assets?

A tax charge applies to the benefit people get from the free or low-cost enjoyment of assets they formerly owned or provided the funds to purchase but have now 'given' away.

The charge applies to both tangible (land, property, possessions, etc.) and intangible assets.

This will primarily affect people who have entered into 'contrived arrangements' to dispose of valuable assets while retaining the ability to use them. This is most frequently encountered in Inheritance Tax avoidance schemes where property is given away but please be aware, this is a charge to Income Tax not Inheritance Tax.

There are specific exceptions to the charge:

- The property ceased to be owned before 18 March 1986.

- The property formerly owned is currently owned by your spouse or civil partner.

- The property was sold at open market value and paid for in cash.

- The asset still forms part of the individual's estate for Inheritance Tax purposes under the gift with reservation rules.

- The asset was only owned by virtue of an inheritance which has subsequently been varied by agreement with the beneficiaries (i.e. a deed of variation).

- Any enjoyment of the asset is incidental, or arises after an out-and-out gift to a family member and comes to the benefit of the donor because of unforeseen changes in the donor's circumstances.

The amount of the tax charge will be based on the rental value for land and property, and five per cent of capital value for possessions and intangible assets, subject to a *de minimis* limit of £5,000.

As it may be impossible to withdraw from potentially complex transactions from the past, an election can be made to have the value of the asset included in the estate for Inheritance Tax purposes. This will avoid an Income Tax charge becoming due. You should take professional advice if you think this applies to you.

CHAPTER 3
National Insurance

What is National Insurance?

National Insurance contributions are an extra and important tax that has to be paid on certain sources of income. The contributions paid are, in principle, used to pay for an individual's following state benefits:

- State Retirement Pension
- Bereavement Allowance
- Bereavement Payment
- Widowed Parent's Allowance
- Maternity Allowance
- Jobseeker's Allowance
- Employment and Support Allowance

What are the different classes of National Insurance?

There are four classes of National Insurance and some have subdivisions.

- **Class 1** primary contributions are paid by employees on their earnings. Secondary contributions are paid by their employers on the same amount. Class 1A contributions are paid by employers on their employees' benefits in kind. (See also 'What National Insurance is payable on employees' benefits?', page 55.) Class 1B contributions are paid by employers where they decide to pay the tax on their employees' benefits under a so-called PAYE Settlement Agreement.

- **Class 2** contributions are paid by the self-employed (but also see Class 4).

- **Class 3** contributions are voluntary. You can pay them in order to protect your benefits, if you are not otherwise paying National Insurance contributions (e.g. this might arise because you have no earnings on which National Insurance is payable, but you still want to pay for a state pension). From October 2015 to 5 April 2017, pensioners who are not eligible for the new single tier pension will be able to purchase additional pension entitlement by paying Class 3A contributions. The cost will vary depending upon the age of the individual. Independent financial advice should be sought on this matter.

- **Class 4** contributions are additional contributions paid by the self-employed, whose earnings exceed a certain sum. Class 4 contributions don't provide any further benefits for the contributor.

You won't have to pay National Insurance contributions if you have retired or have passed normal retirement age. However, if you are still working beyond normal retirement age, your employer remains liable for their Class 1 contributions. In April 2010, the normal retirement age of women started to increase and will rise to 65 by November 2018. From December 2018, the state pension age for both men and women will start to rise, to reach 66 by October 2020, 67 between 2034 and 2036, and 68 between 2044 and 2046.

Who pays what?

National Insurance – the basic facts for 2016/17

1. Employees pay 12 per cent of their earnings between £155 per week and £827 per week, and 2 per cent on all earnings over that figure.

2. Employers pay 13.8 per cent on their employees' earnings over £156 per week. There is no upper limit.

3. The self-employed pay £2.80 per week, which is now collected with the tax liability on 31 January.

4. In addition, self-employed people with profits over £8,060 pay 9 per cent on all profits between £8,060 and £43,000, and 2 per cent on all profits over that figure.

5. Self-employed people with low earnings (less than £5,965 in 2016/17) can elect not to pay National Insurance, but this is not usually a good idea unless contributions are being paid on other sources of income.

6. People over normal retirement age and children under 16 pay nothing. However, employers still have to pay 13.8 per cent on their earnings.

7. If you don't come into any of the above categories (i.e. if you are going abroad), you can elect to pay £14.10 a week in order to maintain your contributions record.

Note: Items 1 and 2 are called Class 1; 3 and 5 are Class 2; 7 is Class 3 and 4 is Class 4.

What do I get for the money I pay in National Insurance?

The table below gives you an indication of what the different classes of National Insurance contributions pay for:

Type of benefit	Class 1 (employed)	Class 2 (self-employed)	Class 3 (voluntary)
State Retirement Pension basic	Yes	Yes	Yes
State Retirement Pension additional	Yes	No	No
New State Pension	Yes	Yes	Yes
Bereavement Benefits	Yes	Yes	Yes
Maternity Allowance	Yes	Yes	No
Contribution-based Employment & Support Allowance	Yes	Yes	No
Contribution-based Jobseeker's Allowance	Yes	No	No

How are National Insurance contributions paid?

- **Class 1** contributions are paid on a weekly or monthly basis by the employer (secondary contributions). The employer deducts its employees' contributions (primary contributions) from their gross pay (along with Income Tax and other deductions) and pays that sum to HMRC, together with its own contributions, by the 19th of the following month.

- **Class 2** contributions have historically been paid by monthly direct debit or quarterly in arrears. From 6 April 2015, they will be included with the self-assessment payments in January and July each year. Therefore, the first payments will be due in January and July 2017 relating to the 2015/16 tax year.

- **Class 3** contributions are usually paid in a lump sum to HMRC.

- **Class 4** contributions are calculated along with the self-employed's self-assessment Income Tax calculation and paid once or twice a year, with the Income Tax payments. (This applies to any Class 4 contribution.)

There are proposals for arrears of Class 2 contributions to be collected via a tax code adjustment for those in employment. There are also proposals for Class 2 contributions to be abolished and for a full review of the Class 4 contributions regime.

How do I find my National Insurance number?

If you don't know your National Insurance number, write to your local Jobcentre (whose address and telephone number you will find in the telephone book) and ask it to give you your National Insurance number, telling it your:

- full name;

- maiden name;

- date of birth;

- date of marriage;
- present address.

If you need to apply for a National Insurance number, you will be asked to attend an interview and prove your identity.

What happens if I should be paying National Insurance contributions but fail to do so?

Make no mistake, this can be expensive either if you start up as an employer who fails to deduct tax and National Insurance contributions from your employees' wages, or if you start in self-employment and fail to register with HM Revenue & Customs (HMRC).

If, as an employer, you fail to pay over the correct National Insurance contributions for your employees by 19 April following the end of the tax year, not only will these have to be paid over, but in addition there will be interest due on the late payment and, in addition to that, there will be penalties for failing to make the payments on time.

If you are an employee whose employer is failing to deduct contributions from your pay and pay them over to HMRC, you cannot be held liable to make the payment yourself. It's the employer's responsibility. Our understanding of the law is that, since it's the employer's responsibility, there is no way in which HMRC can get you to pay the National Insurance contributions that should have been deducted from your gross pay nor should your benefits be affected, because HMRC will collect the contributions from your employer.

HMRC is responsible for National Insurance contributions. The application forms for the newly self-employed are designed in such a way that the National Insurance obligations are dealt with at the same time as registering for tax under self-assessment. Where earnings are below the small earnings exception threshold and you decide that you don't wish to pay contributions (but see 5 on page 31), you must apply for an exception certificate. This can be done at the same time as registration or at any time later.

Where existing self-employed people are not paying the appropriate contributions, they could be made to catch up and the outstanding payments could be subject to interest and penalties. HMRC can claw back contributions without a time limit. Contrast this with the situation where you have been claiming exemption, but realise that you would be better off if you were to pay contributions. As an individual you can only catch up with the last six years of contributions.

Once Class 4 contributions have been calculated on your Tax Return they become part of your overall tax liability and are thereafter no longer separately identified. Unpaid contributions are treated in the same way as unpaid tax.

What should I do if I'm worried that my National Insurance contributions are not up to date?

You should contact the Pensions Service and find out exactly where you stand with regard to contributions you have made and benefits you are entitled to. This is called a retirement pension forecast. You can generally make contributions for the previous 6 years if there are any gaps in your contribution record. The forecast will show you what can be done in this regard and what the impact will be on your pension entitlement.

From 12 October 2015 up until 5 April 2017, it will be possible for people who are eligible for their basic state pension or additional state pension prior to 6 April 2016 (men born before 6 April 1951 and women born before 6 April 1953) to make an payment to HMRC to increase their pension entitlement. It will be possible to increase your pension entitlement by up to £25 per week. There is an online top-up calculator at www.gov.uk/state-pension-topup.

We recommend that everyone who is contemplating making additional payments to increase their pension entitlement takes independent financial advice on the matter.

What is Class 4 National Insurance?

This is the extra National Insurance 'tax' that has to be paid by the self-employed when their earnings exceed a certain threshold. It's an additional tax, and tax is the right word, because it actually buys no further benefits for the payer. It's calculated as part of the self-assessment tax and Class 4 National Insurance calculation and paid with Income Tax on the same dates as Income Tax.

What if I have paid too much National Insurance?

People with either multiple employments or both employment and self-employment no longer have a specific maximum level of contributions. Instead, the legislation provides a formula and each individual will have his own individualised Class 1 and Class 2 maximum figures. Examples of how these maxima are calculated are available on HMRC's website (www.hmrc.gov.uk). Refunds can generally be claimed for the last six contribution years.

If I am self-employed and have not been paying National Insurance, what will happen?

If you are self-employed and are not paying Class 2 National Insurance contributions, you will be found out. The consequences are:

1. You may get a bill for the unpaid contributions.
2. A penalty may be imposed.
3. You could be subject to a criminal prosecution.
4. You are diminishing your entitlement to a state pension.

Do employers have to pay National Insurance contributions on benefits in kind?

Employers are required to pay Class 1A contributions at 13.8 per cent of all benefits, such as company cars and private medical insurance provided to their employees. If they pay their employees' tax on such benefits in accordance with a PAYE Settlement Agreement, they will also have to pay Class 1B contributions on that tax.

National Insurance deferment

You may be concerned that you are going to pay too much National Insurance. This can happen if you have a number of employments or if you have both employments and self-employments. However, just having a number of sources of earned income does not mean that you must have paid too much, just that you might pay too much. It all hinges on the amounts of the earnings and/or profits. Deferment forms can be downloaded from the HMRC website (www.gov.uk/defer-self-employed-national-insurance) and the forms needed are CA72A for Class 1 deferment or CA72B for Class 2 and Class 4 deferment.

CHAPTER 4

Employment and Income Tax

What do I do if I employ somebody?

Taking somebody on can be one of the early big milestones in any business. What follows can also apply to private individuals who are employing people such as cooks, nannies, gardeners, etc. and so, while most of what follows relates to the things that a businessperson should do, private individuals should be aware that they may well be caught by the PAYE regulations that relate to employing people.

There is no easy answer to this very simple question. Having said this, the only answer is that you have to obey the law but knowing what the law is, is not always easy in itself.

If you take on somebody and you are paying him more than £156 a week, no matter what his age*, you have to pay employer's National Insurance contributions and the rate is 13.8 per cent. If this is the case, then the first thing you should do is inform HMRC that you have taken somebody on. You can do this by calling the New Employer Helpline on 0845 607 0143.

The second thing you should do is decide how you are going to handle the PAYE payment obligations. There are three possibilities:

1. Ask a professional accountant or payroll bureau to look after the PAYE side of things for you. Both will tell you how much to pay your employees net of tax and National Insurance each week or month and will also advise you how much your monthly or quarterly payments to HMRC

*From 6 April 2016, there is an exemption from employers' National Insurance for any employees who are under 21 and whose earnings are fewer than £827 per week (£43,000 pa).

are. Each will also be able to help you with the benefit forms (P11Ds).

2. Buy a simple computer program and do the work in-house yourself. These are good, economically priced and well worth the investment in both software and stationery.

3. Use the HMRC website, which has a tax and NIC calculator. The software provided free by HMRC is certainly worth considering but you cannot print out payslips from it.

If you take on someone earning more than £112 per week and less than £155 per week, National Insurance contributions won't be due but you still need to notify HMRC of his pay each week or month, so as to ensure that he qualifies for National Insurance credits. Paying someone over £112 per week also means that you are caught by the real time information regime. This requires the employer to submit electronically pay details to HMRC on or before the date when payments are made to employees. This requirement can be dealt with by most PAYE software, or, if you have fewer than 10 employees, you can use the free software provided on the HMRC website.

If you take on someone earning less than £155 per week, while there may be no National Insurance Contributions to worry about, you may still find that you need to deduct tax from his earnings. This depends on the tax code you have been directed to use, which is either shown on Form P45 ('Details of employee leaving work') from his previous job or on Form P9 ('Notice to Employer of Employee's Tax Code').

We said at the start that there is no easy answer to this. Perhaps the best answer to give you is to discuss the matter with HMRC or with a professional accountant. Make no mistake, it is a complicated business and one that is very important to get right. Employers should not turn a blind eye to their obligations. HMRC also run courses to help employers comply with their obligations. With only a few exceptions, all employers are required to use online filing for PAYE.

Is the person I'm taking on an employee or self-employed?

As with the previous question there is no easy answer to this. There have been many painful cases brought to light by a visiting HMRC PAYE investigator. Business owners who thought that all their people were self-employed have discovered to their horror and great expense that they should have been deducting tax and National Insurance from the gross payments that they have been making to their staff.

Below you will find a list of questions that you should ask which will help you decide whether the person whose services you are using is self-employed or an employee.

As practising accountants we are of the opinion that, if somebody is 'engaged' on a regular basis, but is regarded by both parties as self-employed (and the following questionnaire justifies this decision), a contract for services should be signed by both parties which can be shown to HMRC and which clearly establishes that the arrangement is one of self-employment.

Employed or self-employed? A questionnaire to help you decide

HMRC is keen to classify self-employed people as employees because this increases National Insurance contributions and Income Tax.

How can you tell if someone is an employee or is self-employed? Answering the following questions should help. Note that there are separate and new rules for workers in the construction industry; the following questions are not appropriate for such workers. (On the HMRC website there is an Employment Status Indicator that can be used as a guide, although it may still be worthwhile getting professional advice on the matter.) We must emphasise that these questions give an indication of status. The different points considered carry different weights in the overall decision, so if the overall result is marginal, it would probably be best to seek professional advice on the matter. There are many tax cases where people thought they were self-employed but a court or tribunal found that they were not, with expensive consequences.

1. Is there a contract of service, i.e. a contract of employment?

   A 'no' answer indicates self-employment.

2. Is there a contract for services, i.e. a notice supplied by the person carrying out the work (A), indicating the nature of goods or services he will provide to B (this need not be written)?

A 'yes' answer indicates self-employment.

3. Is the person who does the work in business on his own account?

    A 'yes' answer indicates self-employment.

4. If the person is in business on his own account, has evidence been provided that this is indeed the case (e.g. copy accounts, the payment of Class 2 National Insurance contributions)?

    A 'yes' answer indicates self-employment.

5. Are the hours worked decided by the person doing the work?

    A 'yes' answer indicates self-employment.

6. Are the days worked decided by the person doing the work?

    A 'yes' answer indicates self-employment.

7. Does the person doing the work decide when to take his own holidays?

    A 'yes' answer indicates self-employment.

8. Does the business proprietor supervise the work?

    A 'no' answer indicates self-employment.

9. Is the person part and parcel of the business?

    A 'no' answer indicates self-employment.

10. Does the person supply tools and/or materials when he carries out the work?

    A 'yes' answer indicates self-employment.

11. Does the person doing the work give the business an invoice for the work done?

    A 'yes' answer indicates self-employment.

12. Does the business calculate how much to pay the person doing the work and give a payslip?

    A 'no' answer indicates self-employment.

13. Is self-employment the intention of both parties?

    A 'yes' answer indicates self-employment.

14. Is the person bound by the customer care credo of the business?

    A 'no' answer indicates self-employment.

15. Is the person carrying out the work required to wear a uniform or dress tidily at the diktat of the business?

    A 'no' answer indicates self-employment.

16. Is the person carrying out the work provided with a car or transport by the business?

A 'no' answer indicates self-employment.

17. In the event of sickness, does the business continue to pay the person while not at work?

A 'no' answer indicates self-employment.

18. Is the person carrying out the work at liberty to work for other businesses?

A 'yes' answer indicates self-employment.

19. Is the person carrying out the work required to work in order to perform a specific task?

A 'yes' answer indicates self-employment.

20. Does the business, on asking this person to carry out work for it, assume any responsibility or liability characteristic of an employment, such as employment protection, employees' liability, pension entitlements, etc.?

A 'no' answer indicates self-employment.

21. Is the person who does the work paid an agreed price per job?

A 'yes' answer indicates self-employment (i.e. he is not paid for the hours he works, but for the work carried out).

22. Is the work carried out regularly?

A 'no' answer indicates self-employment.

23. Does the individual work for other people?

A 'yes' answer indicates self-employment.

24. Does the person carrying out the work advertise?

A 'yes' answer indicates self-employment.

25. Does the person carrying out the work have headed stationery?

A 'yes' answer indicates self-employment.

26. Can the person send a substitute? If so, has this ever happened?

A 'yes' answer indicates self-employment.

27. Does the person have to rectify faulty workmanship in his own time and at his own expense?

A 'yes' answer indicates self-employment.

Having addressed these questions, you should now begin to know whether in reality the person under consideration is an employee or is self-employed. However, a definite answer can only be given by the courts and just because a worker is self-employed elsewhere he can still be classed as an employee of yours.

What is PAYE?

PAYE stands for Pay As You Earn. It represents a logical system whereby week by week or month by month an employer deducts tax in such a way that, at the end of the Income Tax year, the right amount of tax has been deducted and handed over to the authorities. It works in the following way:

Let us say that you earn £15,000 a year and your personal allowance is £11,000. Your rate of tax will be 20 per cent.

If you paid your tax just once a year, you would calculate the tax as follows:

- £15,000 less your tax-free personal allowance of £11,000 gives you:

- taxable pay of £4,000 on which:

- tax at 20 per cent is £800.

The way PAYE works is to collect that £800 on a weekly or monthly basis as follows:

Somebody with a tax allowance of £11,000 would be given a PAYE code of 1100. During the year, at whatever payment date you were making a wages or salary payment, an appropriate proportion of that £11,000 would be deducted by your software from the gross pay (in this example, either £211.53 for a weekly paid employee or £916.67 for a monthly paid employee). This would then give the amount to be taxed at 20 per cent. So, for a weekly paid employee, it would be gross £288.46 less £211.53 equals £76.93, to be taxed at 20%. So the PAYE is £15.38; and £15.38 x 52 weeks = £799.76 which is near enough to £800. For a monthly paid employee, it would be gross £1,250.00 less £916.67, equals £333.33 to be taxed at 20%. So the PAYE is £66.66; and £66.66 x 12 = £799.92, which is also near enough to £800.

What is a tax code and what is a notice of coding?

The previous question should give you an answer on your tax code. Regarding a notice of coding (P2), anyone who is being paid through PAYE will be given one. This is a document which is sent to the taxpayer by HMRC explaining how it calculates his tax code. A much simpler document, simply giving the tax code, will be handed to the employer so that he knows which tax code to apply to the employee's pay.

In other words a simple answer is – a tax code is a number given to an individual which enables the employer to work out how much tax to deduct and a notice of coding is the piece of paper on which that number has been printed by the tax authorities.

What if I fail to operate PAYE properly?

This can be very nasty. Employers who fail to operate PAYE properly can find that, when they are found out (and they will be found out!), they have to pay over not only the tax and National Insurance contributions that should have been deducted, as well as the National Insurance contributions that they, as employers, should have been paying, but also interest on the late payment if it was paid after 19 April following the end of the tax year and a penalty of up to 100 per cent of the tax for not having done it properly in the first place.

Don't fail to operate PAYE properly. However, if you discover an innocent error, contact HMRC at once and they will give you guidance on sorting it out.

What records does an employer have to keep?

A proper system for keeping employees' records consists of the following:

For each employee:

•   A contract of employment

- Job description

- Notices of PAYE coding

- A permanent data sheet recording the employee's full name, home address, date of birth, National Insurance number, gender, hours worked, date of joining, dates of pay rises, etc.

Employers certainly have a number of important obligations. Our view is that, if employers are doing their job properly, they will want to keep their records properly, pay their people properly and keep within the law. In our experience it's businesses that behave in such a manner that succeed and flourish.

What is real time information (RTI)?

This is a fairly recent initiative introduced by HMRC, the main purpose of which is to give HMRC accurate and up-to-date information about what employees are earning. It also allows HMRC to ensure that it is receiving from employers the correct amount of tax, National Insurance and any other deductions that are due. It represents a transformation in the way that employers operate their PAYE arrangements and it is claimed (by HMRC) that it will make life easier for employers and will facilitate the implementation of Universal Credits.

Fundamentally, every time an employee is paid the employer must make an electronic submission to HMRC giving details of the employee, the amount paid to them, the deductions made from the payment and also details of the hours the employee has worked.

If you are in business, and have an employee who is paid over £112 per week, you will still be caught by this change in the rules.

All employers need to ensure that they have an accurate record of their employees' full name, home address, gender, date of birth and NI number. Any employees who have left need to be removed from the system, and new employees added so that the record is always fully up to date.

An initial electronic submission needs to be made to HMRC to check that HMRC have the same details for your employees as you do. This allows any errors to be spotted and rectified with either the employer's records or HMRC records.

When the employee data has been aligned with HMRC, approval can then be given for the employer to use the RTI system.

Every time an employee is paid, an electronic report has to be made to HMRC. So, if your employees are paid weekly, there will be reports made every week, but if they are paid monthly, the reports will only be monthly. If an employer pays an employee, but fails to make the appropriate electronic report, the employer will be penalised. This means that businesses will no longer be able to pay 'casual' wages.

When an electronic report has been made, it is not possible to make any changes to these details once the following pay period has been run. If an error has been made, or there is some other reason for needing to change the pay details, this will have to be done in the following pay period. Compliance failures will be penalised in the year ended 5 April 2016 and subsequent years. To help small employers, those businesses having fewer than 10 employees will be able to use the software on the HMRC website in order to make electronic filings to HMRC.

What is the National Minimum Wage?

From 1 April 2016 the National Living Wage has been introduced. This is £7.20 per hour and this is the minimum that must be paid to all employees aged 25 and over. However, there are other rates that you should know, as per the following table.

	From 1 Oct 2015
16- to 17-year-olds	3.87
18- to 20-year-olds	5.30
21- to 24-year-olds	6.70
Apprentice rate	3.30

HMRC is likely to ask you to prove that you are paying at least these rates, so you must keep records. Failure may result in fines of up to £5,000 for each offence. For more information, call the Pay and Work Rights Helpline on 0800 917 2368.

What are Statutory Sick Pay and Statutory Maternity Pay?

The best way of finding the full answer to this particular question is either to visit the government website (www.gov.uk) or refer to Lawpack's book *Employment Law Made Easy*.

However, the principle is that when someone is sick the government expects the employer to pay that person sick pay (Statutory Sick Pay or 'SSP'). From 6 April 2014, the Percentage Threshold Scheme – the reimbursement of some smaller employers for Statutory Sick Pay payments – has ceased. The money saved by this is being used to fund a new Health and Work Service.

Statutory Maternity Pay ('SMP') is also a complicated subject. The same principle applies, namely that the employer pays its employees who are absent to have babies and the government reimburses the payment through the PAYE system.

If you are not eligible for SMP, you may be eligible for Maternity Allowance, which is not taxable.

What tax-deductible expenses can an employee claim?

If you are an employee, which business expenses are deductible for tax purposes and which are not?

There is a general rule that any business expenses must be incurred wholly, exclusively and **necessarily** for the purposes of the business.

Clothes

Normally allowed – The cost of replacing, cleaning and repairing protective clothing (e.g. overalls, boots) and functional clothing (e.g. uniforms) necessary for your job and which you are required to provide. The cost of cleaning protective clothing or functional clothing provided by your employer, if cleaning facilities are not provided.

Not allowed – Ordinary clothes you wear for work (e.g. pinstripe suit) which you could wear outside work – even if you never choose to.

Tools, etc.

Normally allowed – The cost of maintaining and repairing tools and instruments which you are required to provide. From April 2016, the cost of replacing tools has been abolished as an allowable expense. However, claims for the replacement of tools can be made using the Annual Investment Allowance regime, which also covers the purchase of new plant and machinery.

Cost of working at home

Normally allowed – A proportion of lighting, heating, telephone, cleaning, insurance, rent, Council Tax, water rates and mortgage interest, if part of your home is used for business. However, these expenses are only allowed if it's necessary that you carry out your duties at or from home (i.e. if it's an express or implied condition of your employment). If part of your home is used exclusively for work, then this could lead to a Capital Gains Tax liability when you come to sell your home.

Stationery, etc.

Normally allowed – The cost of reference books which are necessary for your job and which you are required to provide. The cost of stationery used strictly for your job.

Not allowed – The cost of books you feel you need to do your job properly but which are, in fact, unnecessary, as well as subscriptions to journals to keep up with general news.

Interest

Normally allowed – The interest on loans to buy equipment (e.g. a personal computer) necessary for the job.

Not allowed – The interest on an overdraft or credit card.

Travelling

Normally allowed – Expenses incurred strictly in the course of carrying out the job. See also 'What are Authorised Mileage Allowance Payments?' on page 52. A company car: if you pay for fuel, you can claim a lower rate of mileage payment (See 'What are advisory fuel rates' on page 51).

Not allowed – Travel from home to your normal place of work.

Accompanying spouses

Normally allowed – The cost of your husband or wife travelling with you if either has, and uses, a practical qualification directly associated with the trip. Often only a proportion of the cost is allowed.

Hotels and meals

Normally allowed – If you keep up a permanent home, reasonable hotel and meal expenses when travelling in the course of your job. In addition, if you stay away overnight while travelling on business, you can claim £5 for incidental expenses to cover private phone calls, laundry and newspapers (£10 per night if you are outside the UK).

Others

Normally allowed – Pension scheme contributions. Professional subscriptions.

What are 'fixed deductions'?

These are flat rate expenses for employees to cover the cost of tools, special clothing, etc. not provided by their employer. The amounts are mostly agreed with trade unions and don't preclude further claims, if justified.

HM Revenue & Customs' (HMRC) website at Employment Income Manual 50000 to 70199 contains a lot of information about particular occupations and the expenses that can be claimed for them. For example, nursing staff (which includes midwives of all grades, auxiliaries, students and assistants) can claim £100 per annum laundry allowance, £12 per annum shoe allowance and £6 per annum stocking allowance. (For male nurses this can include socks.)

What might be the effect on my Council Tax banding if I work from home and use my home as an office?

If you are an employee, so long as your employer agrees that you can work from home (and whether or not your employer provides you with equipment to carry out such work), you may be entitled to seek a reduction in Council Tax on the ground that the room you use as an office can no longer be used, for example as a bedroom. It would be advisable for you not to hold business meetings at your home, because too many of those might constitute a change of use and cause other problems with your local council.

You may be interested to learn that one local council, having reduced the amount of Council Tax payable on such a house, sought to impose business rates on the part of the house used for business purposes. However, it failed in its endeavours and the local valuation office decided not to proceed with the case.

Also, using part of your main residence exclusively for business purposes may jeopardise your eligibility for Principal Private Residence relief, and may create a liability to Capital Gains Tax when you come to sell it.

What is the Working Time Directive?

The Working Time Regulations regulate working hours. The rules cover all workers, full-time and part-time, regardless of the size of firm for which they work and including domestic servants. They extend to quite a few who, for tax purposes, would be counted as self-employed, such as freelancers.

The regulations provide that:

1. workers don't work more than 48 hours a week;

2. night workers don't work more than eight hours a night and are offered regular health assessments;

3. workers have a rest period of 11 consecutive hours between each working day;

4. workers have an in-work rest break of 20 minutes when working more than six hours;

5. workers have at least 5.6 weeks' paid leave each year (including bank holidays).

Only in the case of the 48-hour week may individual workers choose to agree to ignore the regulations and work more than 48 hours. If they do, the agreement must be in writing and must allow the worker to bring the agreement to an end.

There are a number of other flexibilities and a lot of detailed definitions. If you would like to learn more, you can obtain a free copy of the Guide to Working Time Regulations from the Department for Business, Enterprise and Regulatory Reform (BERR).

What about holiday pay?

Holiday pay is not really a tax matter but it can be dealt with under this section.

Holiday pay would normally be specified in a contract of employment and all employees should be issued with a contract of employment by their employer. However, whether holiday pay is paid under a contract or under any other arrangement, it forms part of gross pay and is treated exactly the same as any other pay.

What are the rules about directors and tax?

If you are a company director and your company pays you wages, salary, bonus or commission, you must apply the PAYE procedures.

The Income Tax aspect is calculated in exactly the same way as for an employee, but there is a very important difference in the calculation of the National Insurance contributions. If you are a director, at 6 April you need to use the 'annual earnings period' calculation and if you became a director during the year you must use the 'pro-rata annual earnings period'. It's also possible for HMRC to direct that you use the 'annual earnings period' for certain employees (e.g. for the spouse of a director who gets paid an annual bonus).

What if I provide benefits for my employees?

Any benefits provided for employees must, in the first instance, be regarded as taxable and liable to be reported to HMRC.

The time limit for submitting Forms P9D and P11D to the Tax Office is 6 July following the tax year end.

The Class 1A National Insurance Contribution liability on the employer for any benefits made available to employees is calculated using the P11D information and payment must be made by 19 July. From April 2016 HMRC are introducing a scheme to allow the payrolling of certain benefits. Further details will be announced during the year.

Also, from 6 April 2016 HMRC has introduced a trivial benefits in kind exemption. Provided the conditions are met, a £50 per annum trivial benefit exemption will apply to each employee. Qualifying trivial benefits provided to directors, office holders and members of their household of £300 will also be covered by the exemption.

What are Authorised Mileage Allowance Payments?

Where an employee uses his own vehicle for company purposes, he will obviously look to his employer for reimbursement for his expenses. These are now repaid using the Authorised Mileage Allowance Payment (AMAP) rates, which show the maximum mileage rate that can be paid tax free.

The rates are shown in the table below and are fairly self-explanatory, but the following illustration may help.

If an employee with his own car (of whatever engine size) on which he personally pays all the expenses were to do a total of 15,000 miles in a tax year on company business, he could be paid 45p per mile for the first 10,000 miles (£4,500) and 25p per mile for the next 5,000 miles (£1,250). In total, he could be paid £5,750 tax free.

There is no requirement to show payments on an employee's Form P11D if payments are within AMAP limits. If the employer pays over the limit, the excess must be declared on the P11D.

The employer should require the completion of an expense form to back up the claim that the mileage was for business purposes.

The rules are:

Authorised Mileage Allowance Payments rates

Business mileage since 2014/15	Any size of engine
Up to 10,000 miles	45p
Excess over 10,000 miles	25p

What are advisory fuel rates?

Where an employee provides the fuel for business travel in a company car, he will look to his employer for reimbursement of this expense. HMRC has published advisory fuel rates as follows:

From 1 March 2016

For petrol cars*	1400cc or less	10p
	1401cc to 2000cc	12p
	over 2000cc	19p
For diesel cars	1600cc or less	7p
	1601cc to 2000cc	10p
	over 2000cc	11p
LPG	1400cc or less	7p
	1401cc to 2000cc	8p
	over 2000cc	13p

* Petrol hybrid cars are treated as petrol cars for this purpose.

What are the rules for paying tax on motor cars provided by an employer?

This refers to tax payable by drivers of company cars. It should only concern you if you drive a company car or if you are a director of a company which provides company cars to its employees. This doesn't concern anyone who is self-employed.

In effect, Income Tax payable is assessed on a multiple of the level of CO_2 emitted and the list price of a new car.

So the more the CO_2 and the more expensive the car, the higher the tax bill. Company car drivers of small, environmentally friendly cars get the best deal.

Every case should be judged on its merits, so look before you leap. Your company should be able to assist you with transfer of ownership, arranging favourable terms of purchase and/or finance.

What is the tax on employees' vans?

If you are an employee and are provided with a company van you have to pay tax on it if you make private use of it. If you have the van mainly for work journeys and the only private use is commuting, there is no tax to pay. If there is other private use, tax is payable unless this private use is insignificant. HMRC states that:

Private use is insignificant if:

- it is very much the exception to the normal use;

- it is intermittent and irregular; and

- it lasts only for short periods of time on odd occasions during the year.

Examples of insignificant use include an employee who:

- takes an old mattress or other rubbish to the tip once or twice a year;

- regularly makes a slight detour to drop off a child at school or stops at a newsagent on the way to work; calls at the dentist on the way home from work.

Examples of use which is **not** insignificant include an employee who:

- regularly uses the van to do the supermarket shopping;
- takes the van away on a week's holiday;
- uses the van outside of work for social activities.

What are the car benefit charges based on CO_2 emissions for 2016/17?

CO_2 emissions in grams per kilometre	Tax is based on the following percentage of the price of the car*
2016/17	%
0-50	7
51-75	11
76-94	15
95-99	16
100-104	17
105-109	18
110-114	19
115-119	20
120-124	21
125-129	22
130-134	23
135-139	24
140-144	25
145-149	26
150-154	27
155-159	28
160-164	29

CO_2 emissions in grams per kilometre	Tax is based on the following percentage of the price of the car*
2016/17	**%**
165-169	30
170-174	31
175-179	32
180-184	33
185-189	34
190-194	35
195-199	36
200 and over	37

* Diesels pay a 3% surcharge on all engine sizes, with a maximum payable of 37%.

What are the fuel benefit charges?

Where an employer pays for the car's private fuel, the taxable benefit is the appropriate percentage from the above table applied to £22,200.

Can I get dispensation for travel and subsistence payments?

Most employers will have had the annual chore of having to complete the dreaded Form P11D dealing with employees' benefits.

Although it's not possible to avoid making Tax Returns for genuine benefits (including company cars), it's possible to apply for dispensation from reporting travel and subsistence payments made to employees, so long as some fairly innocuous conditions can be met (receipts are requested, expenses are incurred in the course of business, mileage rates are within HMRC's guidelines and all claims are checked by a senior employee). However, following the recent Budget, the government is working through amending this requirement, so that employers will no longer need to obtain dispensations.

What is auto-enrolment?

Automatic enrolment in a workplace pension. As a strategy to encourage employees to save for their retirement the government requires that employers provide access to a pension scheme and automatically enrol all eligible employees into it. Once enrolled, employees can opt out; however, the employer has a duty to automatically enrol them back in at regular intervals.

The scheme is being phased in from October 2012 for the largest employers through to April 2017 for the smallest. New employers (those from 1 April 2012 onwards) will join the scheme between May 2017 and February 2018.

The scheme dictates that both employer and employee must contribute a minimum percentage of the employee's salary into the pension scheme.

Timing (staging date)	Employee minimum	Employer minimum
October 2012 to April 2018	1%	1%
October 2017 to April 2019	3%	2%
April 2019 onwards	5%	3%

The pension contributions will be payable by the employee on salaries in excess of the personal allowance. Employers will have to contribute on salaries between £5,824 and £43,000 in the year ended 5th April 2017. All employers will be contacted by HMRC in advance of their staging date and we understand that there is some limited provision to delay the staging dates beyond the dates quoted above.

What are the rules if I provide shares and share options for my employees?

Under the All Employee Share Ownership Plan (AESOP), employees may allocate part of their salary to shares in their employer company ('partnership shares') without paying tax or National Insurance contributions, nor are employers' National Insurance contributions payable. Employers may also give free shares to employees, including extra free shares for employees who have partnership shares ('matching shares'), and the cost of the shares and of running the scheme are tax deductible. There are maximum limits of £1,800 worth of partnership shares per year and £3,600 worth of free shares per year, although employers may set lower limits. **Note:** All types of share issued to employees must be reported to HMRC on Form 42 ('Employment-related securities') within 30 days; failure to so do means a fine of £300 per employee.

If the employee takes shares out of the scheme within five years, he is taxed on them. If the shares remain in the scheme for five years or more, they are free of tax and National Insurance contributions when they are withdrawn.

There are two types of share option scheme: 'Save As You Earn' (SAYE)-linked share option schemes and Company Share Option Plans. Under an SAYE scheme, contributions of between £5 and £500 per month are paid under a SAYE contract with a building society or bank. The option will normally be able to be exercised after three, five or seven years when the contract ends. No charge to Income Tax arises on the difference between cost and market value when a share option is exercised, nor at the time it's granted.

The scheme enables an option to be granted now to acquire shares at today's price. The price at which the option may be exercised must not normally be less than 80 per cent of the market value of the shares at the time the option is granted.

Under approved non-savings-related share option schemes, the option must not be granted at a discount and the total market value of shares that may be acquired under the option must not exceed £30,000. If these conditions are complied with, there is no tax charge when options are granted. Nor is there a tax charge when the option is exercised, providing options under the scheme are exercised between three and ten years after they are granted, and not more frequently than once in three years.

What are the different schemes for providing shares for employees?

The different approved schemes are:

- Share Incentive Plans (SIP): Under this scheme, which is also known as an AESOP (All Employee Share Ownership Plan):

- Employers can give up to £3,600 worth of shares to each employee.

- Employees can buy up to £1,800 worth of shares and, under such circumstances, employers can reward the purchasers with two free shares for each share purchased.

- Savings Related Share Options Schemes (SRSOS):

  - Participants can save up to £500 per month to acquire shares at the end of a three-, five- or seven-year period.

- Enterprise Management Incentive (EMI):

  - Companies with gross assets not exceeding £30 million can grant tax and National Insurance Contribution-advantaged share options worth up to £100,000 to any number of employees who work more than 25 hours per week in the business, subject to a total value of £3 million.

- Company Share Option Plans (CSOP):

  - Up to £30,000 of options each can be granted to any number of employees with tax and National Insurance Contribution advantages.

- Schemes outside HMRC's approved range of schemes:

  - These will suffer tax and National Insurance contributions.

Needless to say, professional advice must be sought. For example, shares must not be issued at less than market value. In the case of unapproved schemes, the company makes up its own rules. For these, there is even more need for professional advice because if things go wrong, it can be both embarrassing and expensive.

What are employee-owner shareholders?

The government has created a new employee status, that of 'employee-owner shareholder'. (There seems to be a lot of scope for confusion where you can have employees who are also shareholders.)

These employees will have fewer employee rights than normal employees, but by way of compensation for this will be entitled to receive at least £2,000 of shares in the company that they work for.

The legislation also exempts £2,000 of these shares from an Income Tax and National Insurance charge, which would usually arise if an employer gave shares to an employee. Furthermore, gains of up to £50,000 on the disposal of shares will be exempt from Capital Gains Tax.

What National Insurance is payable on employees' benefits?

If you are an employer and you complete Form P11D for any of your employees, it's likely that there will be a Class 1A National Insurance liability arising on the benefits.

The amount of Class 1A National Insurance contributions payable is calculated by reference to the value of the benefits provided and the application of the Class 1A percentage rate in force, currently 13.8 per cent. Calculation of the Class 1A National Insurance Contribution liability will be possible from the information contained in the P11D Form. Payment of the Class 1A National Insurance contributions will be due by 19 July following the end of the year in question, i.e. 19 July 2016 for 2016/17.

Reading HMRC's employers' guide CWG5(2015) is recommended and this also contains details of further sources of information.

What do employers and employees have to do at the year end?

Employer

The vast majority of employers should now be filing under the real time information (RTI) regime and therefore the following aspects will not apply to them as they have already supplied this information to HMRC as they have gone along. You will not have to submit either P14s or a P35 to HMRC for the year 2015/16.

If there are any employers who have not used the RTI system for the entirety of the 2015/16 tax year, they must complete Forms P14 and Form P35.

All employers, regardless of whether or when RTI has been implemented, will still have an obligation to provide their employees with a P60 for the year and also a P11D form as appropriate. The employer must also ensure that all payments of PAYE tax and National Insurance contributions have been paid over to HMRC and any Class 1A National Insurance contributions due for the year will subsequently be payable. The deadlines for these various items are as follows:

Month 12 payment to HMRC to avoid interest	19 April
Submitting the P14 and P35 to the Tax Office	19 May
Providing the P60 to your employee	31 May
Submitting Forms P11D to the Tax Office	6 July
Making the Class 1A National Insurance contributions payment to HMRC	19 July

Employee

You should keep your P60 in a safe place. You should keep evidence of any income that you have received during the year and any tax that you have paid. This is not limited to your employment and includes all of your tax affairs.

What are the rules for charitable giving through the PAYE system?

If an employer participates in the Payroll Giving scheme ('Give As You Earn'), an employee can authorise the deduction of whatever sum he chooses from his earnings before tax, for passing on to charities chosen by him, through a charity agency with which the employer has made an arrangement. The employee thus receives full tax relief for the contributions made.

What tax is payable on payments for compensation for loss of office?

Compensation for loss of office and wages in lieu of notice are both taxable when provided for in the terms and conditions of the employment. Payments of deferred earnings are also taxable under the normal PAYE rules.

Provided that the payment is not caught by the normal PAYE rules, the first £30,000 of the redundancy payment is exempt from tax. Any surplus received over and above this is treated as earnings and PAYE applied in the normal way.

Statutory redundancy payments are included within the £30,000 exemption.

Payments for death or disability in service are not taxable. Lump sums received under approved pension schemes are also exempt from tax.

What are the tax rules if I'm employed outside the UK?

If your employment abroad is full-time, spans a complete tax year and you actually carry out all your duties abroad, you are normally treated by concession as a non-resident from the date of leaving until the date of return. If you don't attain non-resident status, you will be a UK resident throughout.

There has been a number of tax cases involving residence issues, and the whole area is becoming increasingly complex, with HMRC taking a much tougher line on residence status. It is therefore recommended that professional advice is sought. A statutory residence test has been introduced from 6 April 2013. More details can be found in chapter 13.

What is Employment Allowance?

From 6 April 2016, eligible employers will be able to reduce the amount of Employers Class 1 NIC they have to pay by up to £3,000 (£2,000 in the 2015/16 tax year). This is a generous allowance which will benefit the vast majority of employers. It is likely that most mainstream PAYE software will simply require a tick in a box in order to claim this automatically.

Businesses, charities and Community Amateur Sports Clubs can claim the allowance. The term 'businesses' includes sole traders, partnerships and companies. In the 2015 Budget, it was announced that people who employ their own carers will be eligible to claim Employment Allowance in the year commencing 6 April 2015. There are however some exclusions; you cannot claim Employment Allowance if you:

- employ someone for personal, household or domestic affairs e.g. nanny, au pair, housekeeper, gardener, chauffeur, etc.

- already claim the allowance through a connected business;

- are a public authority;

- are the sole director and employee of your own limited company;

- carry out functions either wholly or mainly of a public nature – unless you have charitable status.

Examples of this are NHS services, GP services, providing services to the public on behalf of the local council etc. There is more information at www.hmrc.gov.uk/nicsemploymentallowance

Service companies (as defined for IR35) are not able to claim the allowance in respect of deemed payments of employment income. Please be aware that the term service company does have a very specific meaning, and is not simply a company which provides a service, e.g. accountancy.

If you do not use suitable software for online filing then you can still claim the Employment Allowance at the beginning of the tax year using a paper Employer Payment Summary. It is also possible to make a claim in the future for relief in the 2014/15 and 2015/16 tax years.

CHAPTER 5

Pensions and tax

What are the general rules on pension contributions and tax?

1. If you wish, you can save in more than one pension scheme at the same time.

2. There is no limit on the amount of money you can save in a pension scheme or the number of pension schemes you can save in – although there are limits on the amount of tax relief you can get.

3. You will get tax relief on contributions up to 100 per cent of your annual earnings (up to an annual allowance set at £40,000 in 2015/16 and 2016/17). However, from April 2016, for those with earnings over £150,000 per annum, the amount of pension contributions upon which tax relief can be claimed is tapered down from £40,000 to £10,000. So if you put a net contribution of £100 into your pension scheme, the government will put in another £25 so that your gross contribution is £125.

4. If you are a higher or additional rate taxpayer, you will get extra tax relief on the gross contribution of £125 (£25 in the case of a 40 per cent taxpayer and £31.25 in the case of a 45 per cent taxpayer).

5. Even if you are not a taxpayer, you can still get tax relief on pension contributions. You can put in up to £2,880 in any one tax year and the

government will top this up with another £720 – giving you total pension savings with tax relief of £3,600 per year.

6. The rules about retirement are flexible. You can continue working while drawing your pension, where the scheme rules allow it.

7. If your scheme rules allow, you can take up to 25 per cent of your pension fund as a tax-free lump sum.

8. If your pension pot is more than the 'lifetime allowance' when you come to take your pension, you may be subject to a tax charge at that time. But this will only apply if your total pension savings are in excess of £1 million from 6 April 2016.

9. You cannot take a pension before you are 55, although you can retire early due to poor health.

10. Very significant changes have been introduced in the March 2014 Budget affecting the access people will have to their pension funds. These changes have come into effect from April 2015 and broadly speaking, people can now access their pension funds without having to purchase an annuity. However, it is strongly recommended that anyone who may be becoming eligible to draw their pension should take professional advice on their options.

11. A number of changes to the current rules came into effect on 27 March 2014, allowing people to have greater freedom and choice over accessing their defined contribution pension savings at retirement. The changes are:

   • reducing the amount of guaranteed income people need in retirement to access their savings flexibly, from £20,000 to £12,000;

   • increasing the amount of total pension savings that can be taken as a lump sum, from £18,000 to £30,000;

   • increasing the capped drawdown withdrawal limit from 120 per cent to 150 per cent of an equivalent annuity;

   • increasing the maximum size of a small pension pot which can be taken as a lump sum (regardless of total pension wealth) from £2,000 to £10,000, and increasing the number of personal pots that can be taken under these rules from two to three.

12. In the 2015 Budget, it was announced that from April 2016 those who had already purchased an annuity can sell that income stream

to a third party. This would generate a cash lump sum which can be taken immediately or drawn down over a period of time.

Is it worth paying into a pension scheme?

There is no straightforward answer to this question. Over the years of our being in practice, we have discovered that clients save towards their retirement in a number of different ways. Some don't wish to pay into a pension scheme, preferring to invest on their own, through either property or other types of investment. This route doesn't suit everyone and we encourage our clients to make sure that they are fully aware of the associated risks before pursuing such a strategy.

For many, the discipline of saving on a regular basis for their retirement appeals along with the attraction of tax relief on contributions and the virtually tax-free growth that can be enjoyed while their money is invested.

Whichever route our clients take, there are obviously charges to consider. For pensions this could be fees paid to an adviser, while for property purchase it might be legal fees such as Stamp Duty, solicitor's costs, etc.

What are SIPPs?

SIPPs are Self Invested Personal Pensions and they allow individuals direct control over the investments in their pension scheme. They provide maximum flexibility in the timing of contributions into, and benefit payments from, the scheme.

An example of such flexibility is that a SIPP allows for up to 25 per cent of the fund to be withdrawn tax free between the ages of 55 and 75. The balance then can be used to provide income for the rest of the individual's life.

SIPPs also provide an attraction for Inheritance Tax purposes because if the individual dies before retirement, the whole of the value of the SIPP is excluded from the deceased's estate.

There are many assets that can be included in a SIPP but some are specifically excluded (e.g. residential property, works of art, fine wines and vintage cars).

One advantage of a SIPP is the opportunity it provides for investing in smaller companies. Another is that a SIPP can borrow up to 50 per cent of its value.

Some individuals who invest in a SIPP opt for the management to be handled at the discretion of an investment management company. One advantage of this is the clear reporting and administrative package that usually comes with such management.

The SIPP market is growing.

What amount of state pension can I expect?

If you ring up the Pension Service (tel 0845 300 0168) and give it your National Insurance number, it should be able to send you a forecast of your anticipated state pension at retirement, which it will work out based on your age and contributions. You can also complete a State Pension Statement request form (BR19), which is available online. A single-tier state pension has been introduced in April 2016 and the full rate is £155.65 per week.

When will I be entitled to my pension?

The pension ages for women are increasing. The table below shows how they are each affected.

If you were born between these dates			Your state pension date will be	Your retirement age will be between
6 April 1952	to	5 May 1952	6 May 2014	62y 0m–62y 1m
6 May 1952	to	5 June 1952	6 July 2014	62y 1m–62y 2m
6 June 1952	to	5 July 1952	6 Sept 2014	62y 2m–62y 3m
6 July 1952	to	5 August 1952	6 Nov 2014	62y 3m–62y 4m
6 August 1952	to	5 Sept 1952	6 January 2015	62y 4m–62y 5m
6 Sept 1952	to	5 October 1952	6 March 2015	62y 5m–62y 6m
6 October 1952	to	5 Nov 1952	6 May 2015	62y 6m–62y 7m
6 Nov 1952	to	5 Dec 1952	6 July 2015	62y 7m–62y 8m
6 Dec 1952	to	5 January 1953	6 Sept 2015	62y 8m–62y 9m
6 January 1953	to	5 February 1953	6 Nov 2015	62y 9m–62y 10m

6 February 1953	to 5 March 1953	6 January 2016	62y 10m–62y 11m
6 March 1953	to 5 April 1953	6 March 2016	62y 11m–63y 0m
6 April 1953	to 5 May 1953	6 July 2016	63y 0m–63y 3m
6 May 1953	to 5 June 1953	6 November 2016	63y 3m–63y 6m
6 June 1953	to 5 July 1953	6 March 2017	63y 6m–63y 9m
6 July 1953	to 5 August 1953	6 July 2017	63y 9m–64y 0m
6 August 1953	to 5 September 1953	6 November 2017	64y 0m–64y 3m
6 September 1953	to 5 October 1953	6 March 2018	64y 3m–64y 6m
6 October 1953	to 5 November 1953	6 July 2018	64y 6m–64y 9m
6 November 1953	to 5 December 1953	6 November 2018	64y 9m–65y 0m

From this point on, men's and women's state pension ages are unified. However, the state pension age then increases for both sexes to 66 in the period November 2018 to October 2020.

The state pension age then increases to 67 for those born between 6 April 1960 and 5 April 1969. This change is to be implemented between 2034 and 2036. There are further plans to increase the state pension age to 68, which are scheduled to be implemented between 2044 and 2046.

Do I have to draw my pension when I reach pension age?

Whether you have yet to start receiving your state pension or are already receiving it, it is possible to defer payment. This can be advantageous if you reach pension age but are continuing to work. It may be that claiming your pension would make you liable to higher rates of tax, for example.

If receipt of your pension is deferred, you can gain an increase in your pension of one per cent for every five weeks of deferral.

If you put off claiming your pension for at least 12 continuous months, you can choose to receive your pension at the normal rate plus a one-off lump sum. This lump sum is taxable, but you may be able to have it paid in a year when you are liable to lower rates of tax than if you had not deferred it.

As you are forgoing your pension now for additional pension later, there is a strong investment aspect to the decision. It is therefore recommended that you take advice on the matter from an independent financial adviser.

CHAPTER 6

Self-employment and partnerships

Should I tell the taxman if I'm going self-employed or starting a partnership?

When you begin self-employment it's very important that somebody (you or your accountant) tells HM Revenue & Customs (HMRC) that you have begun in business, partly so that the correct tax can be paid on time and partly so that the appropriate National Insurance contributions are paid. Anyone beginning self-employment or a partnership must register with HMRC within three months from the end of the month in which the self-employment commenced. Failure to meet this deadline can result in a £100 penalty.

If you are using a paper form rather than online, it is form CWF1 that you need to complete. From 6 April 2015, Class 2 National Insurance contributions are being collected via self-assessment payments on account. Therefore, the use of forms CA5601, which used to be used to pay Class 2 NICs by direct debit, will no longer apply. If you are a partner in a partnership, there are two forms which you should complete for the tax authorities, SA400 Registering a partnership for Self Assessment and SA401 Registering a partner for Self Assessment. Do bear in mind that if your profits or share of profits for 2016/17 are below £5,965 you may claim exemption from paying Class 2 contributions. As we have said before (on page 31), this is only sensible if you have other earnings on which you are paying National Insurance contributions.

Self-employment worries can be taken care of (and avoided) if you choose an accountant to handle your accounts and to advise you about the resulting tax liabilities.

What is trading?

It's sometimes difficult to know if an activity is taxable or not. Typical (in other words difficult) questions might be as follows:

- If I earn £300 a year from self-employed activities, does the taxman want to know?

- My daughter, who is still at school, earns £50 a week from singing in local pubs; does the taxman want to know?

- I occasionally do small jobs for people, being paid in cash; will the taxman want to know?

It's always difficult to give the right answer because, while we know that under law if you are earning money the taxman will want to know, even if there is no tax to be paid, there is that famous maxim, which we cover elsewhere in this book, *de minimis non curat lex,* which means 'the law is not concerned with trifles'. From April 2017, there will be some clarity from HMRC: people earning up to £1,000 from occasional jobs will no longer need to declare or pay tax on this income.

Trading is earning money from an activity. Trading involves not only the earning of the money but also the expenses in achieving that income. Our advice to clients is: use the template we show in Appendix 3 and see if you have made a taxable sum from the activity. If you have, you should report it. Your conscience will tell you if you should be reporting it.

When an activity is in the grey area of being between non-reportable and reportable, each case has to be taken on its merits and decisions arrived at accordingly. However, in principle, once one is trading (earning money from an activity) proper records should be kept and HMRC should be told.

How do I calculate my taxable income from trading?

Basically, you have to take your income and deduct from it all your legitimate business-related expenses. You will see the type of expenses that you can claim in Appendix 3 and in more detail below. However, do bear in mind that some expenses, for instance motoring, may well involve an element of private use. You should only claim that element that relates to the business activity against your trading receipts. It may be that you should only claim a third of your motoring costs against your business. Perhaps a quarter of your Council Tax and insurance costs. Whatever it is, if you have any difficulties in deciding, either go and see a local accountant or visit the Tax Office to discuss it.

A template to help you prepare your figures for the self-employed part of the Tax Return is provided at Appendix 3.

What expenses can I claim?

There is a general rule that any business expenses must be incurred wholly and exclusively for the purposes of the business. This means that some expenses will fall foul of the so-called dual purpose rule. For example, if you attend a business conference in Spain and tack a holiday on the end, your trip will have a dual purpose and the expenses won't be allowed. However, according to HMRC, 'in practice some dual purpose expenses include an obvious part which is for the purposes of the business. We usually allow the deduction of a proportion of expenses like that', and they go on to give the example of car or van expenses.

Basic costs and general running expenses

Normally allowed – The cost of goods bought for resale and raw materials used in business. Advertising, delivery charges, heating, lighting, cleaning, rates, telephone. The rent of business premises. Small tools and special clothing. Postage, stationery, relevant books and magazines. Accountants' fees. Bank charges on business accounts. Fees to professional bodies. Security expenditure.

Not allowed – The initial cost of machinery, vehicles, equipment – but you can claim Annual Investment Allowances, and where the limit for this has been exceeded, capital allowances, on these and so-called 'integral features'. The cost of buildings. Providing for anticipated expenses in the future.

Use of home for work

Normally allowed – The business proportion of telephone calls and line rental, lighting, heating, cleaning, insurance, rent, Council Tax and mortgage interest. Provided you don't use any part of your home exclusively for business purposes, you won't lose your entitlement to private residence relief for Capital Gains Tax.

Wages and salaries

Normally allowed – Wages, salaries, redundancy and leaving payments paid to employees. Pensions for past employees and their dependants. Staff training.

Not allowed – Your own wages or salary or that of any business partner. Your own drawings.

Tax and National Insurance

Normally allowed – Employer's National Insurance contributions for employees. Reasonable pay for your spouse, provided he is actually employed.

Not allowed – Income Tax. Capital Gains Tax. Inheritance Tax. Your own National Insurance contributions.

Entertaining

Normally allowed – Entertainment of own staff (e.g. a Christmas party).

Not allowed – Any other business entertaining.

Pre-trading

Normally allowed – Revenue business expenditure incurred within seven years before starting to trade.

Gifts

Normally allowed – Gifts costing up to £50 a year to each person so long as the gift advertises your business (or things it sells). Gifts (whatever their value) to employees.

Not allowed – Food, drink, tobacco or vouchers for goods given to anyone other than employees.

Travelling

Normally allowed – Hotel and travelling expenses on business trips. Travel between different places of work. The running costs of your own car – whole of cost if used wholly for business, proportion if used privately too.

Not allowed – Travel between home and business. The cost of buying a car or van (but you can claim capital allowances).

Leased cars with CO_2 emissions of more than 130g/km will have 15 per cent of the leasing payments disallowed. There is no restriction for cars with CO_2 emissions of less than or equal to 130g/km.

Interest payments

Normally allowed – The interest on overdrafts and loans for business purposes.

Not allowed – The interest on capital paid or credited to partners.

Hire purchase

Normally allowed – Interest element of instalments (i.e. not the capital cost).

Not allowed – Capital element of instalments (but you may get capital allowances).

Hiring

Normally allowed – Reasonable charge for hire of capital goods, including cars.

Insurance

Normally allowed – Business insurance (e.g. employer's liability, fire and theft, motor, insuring employees' lives).

Not allowed – Your own life insurance.

Trademarks

Normally allowed – Fees paid to register a trademark, design or patent.

Not allowed – The cost of buying a patent from someone else (but you may get capital allowances).

Legal costs

Normally allowed – The costs of recovering debts, defending business rights, preparing service agreements, appealing against rates, renewing a lease for a period not exceeding 50 years (but not if a premium is paid).

Not allowed – Expenses (including Stamp Duty) for acquiring land, buildings or leases. Fines and other penalties for breaking the law, for example parking/speeding fines.

Repairs

Normally allowed – Normal repairs and maintenance to premises or equipment.

Not allowed – The cost of additions, alterations, improvements (but you may get capital allowances).

Debts

Normally allowed – Specific provisions for debts and debts written off.

Not allowed – General reserve for bad or doubtful debts.

Subscriptions

Normally allowed – Payments which secure benefits for your business or staff. Payments to societies that have arrangements with HMRC (in some cases only a proportion).

Not allowed – Payments to political parties, churches and charities (but small gifts to local churches and charities may be allowed).

Travelling and subsistence expenses and tax

Expenses	Employer	Self-employed	Can VAT (Input Tax) be reclaimed?
	Where expenses are incurred by the employer, whether a self-employed trader, a partnership or a company	Where a self-employed trader incurs these expenses on his own behalf	
Entertaining own staff	Allowable	Allowable	Yes*

Expenses	Employer	Self-employed	Can VAT (Input Tax) be reclaimed?
Business travel between place of business and customers, etc. (but not home)	Allowable	Allowable	Yes
Hotel bills, etc.	Allowable	Allowable	Yes, so long as it's billed to the VAT-registered trader
Drinks and meals away from home:			
1. Working/ selling	Allowable	Not allowable	Yes*
2. On training course	Allowable	Allowable	Yes*
3. Buying, trips, etc.	Allowable	Allowable	Yes*
Entertaining business clients	Not allowable	Not allowable	No
Car parking	Allowable	Allowable	Yes
Trade show expenses	Allowable	Allowable	Yes
Fuel	Allowable	Allowable (business proportion only)	Yes**

*   But not if there is any measurable degree of business entertainment.

**   But if the input VAT is reclaimed, remember to include the scale charge in your output tax on the VAT Return.

Can I pay myself?

The answer to this is 'no'. If you look at this logically, you will see how the answer can only be 'no'. If you were to pay yourself a salary out of your self-employment or partnership income, you would have to include the salary as employment income elsewhere on your Tax Return and thereby you would achieve nothing.

Under this section you could also consider whether you could pay your spouse. If he plays a part in the business and has no other income, then there might well be tax to save by paying him for the work that he does.

What is the tax significance of holding trading stock?

If you are running a business that involves the buying and selling of items of stock, at the end of your trading year you have to add up the cost of any unsold stock and deduct it from the cost of your purchases acquired during the year. The reason for this is that those stocks are going to be sold in the following accounting period and therefore you only take advantage of the tax relief that goes with buying those stocks in the year or period in which they are sold. In other words any stocks that you deduct from your cost of sales at the end of your trading period should be added to the costs that you incur in the following year, so that you claim the deduction in the correct year. If you think that your stock may not sell for what you paid for it or it's slow moving, you can write it down to what is called 'net realisable value'.

What is the tax significance of work in progress?

If you have been working on a long contract, the duration of which straddles the end of your accounting period, you are likely to have incurred costs in terms of labour and materials at the end of your year which relate to that contract and which you have not been paid for. Accordingly, you should value those materials, as well as those hours and, as with stocks, carry the sum forward to the following year so as to take advantage of those costs in the year in which you bill your customer for the work.

Do remember that, in assessing the value of work in progress, if you are a partner or a sole proprietor in a business, you don't need to include your own time. However, you do need to include materials.

If you have reached a point where you are entitled to be paid for the work done, then instead of carrying forward that work in progress at cost, an appropriate amount of income should be included at selling price. This is a complicated area and we do recommend that you take advice from either HMRC or a chartered accountant.

What are debtors and what do I do about them?

Debtors are your customers who owe you money. Even though you have not been paid, these amounts must be included in your sales and in your balance sheet. If any of them have subsequently proved to be bad or look doubtful (i.e. you are not going to be paid or you may not be paid), you can claim as an expense a figure relating specifically to the ones that are not going to be, or may not be, paid.

Come the next accounting period, and when that cash comes in, you don't pay tax on that money, because it has already been taxed in the previous year.

What are creditors and what do I do about them?

Creditors are like debtors but the other way round: they are the suppliers to whom you owe money. You are allowed to include amounts owing in your accounts, and get the tax relief for them in the year to which they relate. However, when you come to pay them in the following year, you won't be entitled to tax relief in that year because you have already got the tax relief in the previous year.

What are capital allowances?

You are unable to claim the depreciation charged in your accounts as a tax deduction. Instead, you have to claim, and in a prescribed way, HMRC's own version of depreciation which it calls 'capital allowances'.

You will almost certainly need professional help to do this properly. These allowances are specifically allowed as a deduction against your taxable profits. You can claim capital allowances as follows:

	First-year allowance % that can be claimed by any business	Writing down allowance % of balance that can be claimed
Plant	Nil	18%
Machinery	Nil	18%
Vans	Nil	18%
Patents	Nil	18%
Know-how (a kind of intellectual property)	Nil	25%
Information and Communications Technology	Nil	18%
Computers	Nil	18%
Digital TV	Nil	18%
Websites	Nil	18%
Energy-saving, and water-saving plant and machinery[1]	100%	Nil
Most cars	Nil	18%[2]
Some cars with low CO_2 emissions less than 97 g/km	100%	Nil
Special rate pool[3]	Nil	8%

[1] See the Energy Technology List at http://etl.decc.gov.uk/etl for details of the equipment which will qualify for the 100% First Year Allowance.

[2] For cars with CO_2 emissions above 130g/km the rate is 8 per cent. For cars with CO_2 emissions less than or equal to 130g/km the rate is 18 per cent.

[3] This includes long life assets, integral features, certain thermal insulation and some cars.

What is the Annual Investment Allowance?

This is a capital allowance that allows you to write off the full cost of qualifying plant and equipment – but not cars – in the year of purchase. From 1 April 2014 (for companies, and 6 April 2014 for individuals) until 31 December 2015, expenditure of up to £500,000 on plant, machinery, long life assets and integral features will be relieved in full against profits. This threshold is reduced to £200,000 with effect from 1 January 2016. Any expenditure above this limit will be relieved using the normal capital allowance rules. Where an accounting period spans 1 January the amount of allowance changes on that date, then the periods on each side of that date form two separate allowances for expenditure, each reduced pro rata. This can be something of a trap if you (reasonably) expect that you can add these two bits together. Accounting periods which are less than, or greater than, 12 months will get an increased or a reduced allowance, so long as the amount of allowance during that period does not change.

Where the written down value of the plant and machinery pool is £1,000 or less, this can be written off in full if desired. Many small businesses – especially those which are labour rather than capital intensive, as are many service businesses – are able to claim 100 per cent of their capital expenditure in the year in which they make it.

What are long life assets and what allowances do they get?

Long life assets are items of plant or machinery which are expected to last at least 25 years. The writing down allowance for them is eight per cent. A new 'pool' is created to include long life assets and integral features. Integral features include electrical systems, cold water systems, heating systems, air conditioning, lifts and escalators.

Is there any special tax treatment for farmers?

There are two specific ways in which farmers get special tax treatment:

1. **The herd basis.** The principle of the herd basis is that, because a herd, or a flock for that matter, consists of breeding animals (cows, bulls, rams, ewes), instead of treating these as animals that you will ultimately sell as meat, you treat them as capital assets and not as a revenue item. This book on tax is not the place to describe this particular feature, but the effect of claiming the herd basis at a time of rising animal values is that, when you come to sell those animals (perhaps retire), a substantial part of the sale proceeds won't be subject to tax.

    How should farmers value their stock? Farm stocks and farm animals that are not part of a herd or flock should be valued at the lower of cost or net realisable value. In a number of cases 'cost' will be easy to calculate, but what about animals that have grown considerably since they were bought, animals that have been home bred and crops? For such stocks where it's just not possible to calculate an appropriate 'cost' figure, HMRC allows farmers to use a percentage of market value at the valuation date. These are:

    *   Cattle: 60%

    *   Sheep and pigs: 75%

    *   Deadstock: 75%

2. **Averaging.** From April 2016, because farm results can fluctuate, farmers are able to claim the averaging of profits of any five-year period of assessment, provided they do so within broadly 22 months of the end of the fifth year. As with the herd basis, the rules can be quite complicated, but the effect of claiming for averaging is that you can collectively pay less tax than you would if you had high profits attracting higher rates of tax in one year and lower profits in the adjacent year.

Is there any special tax treatment for Lloyd's insurance underwriters?

Yes, there is special treatment for Lloyd's underwriters. It's such a complicated set of rules, allowances and regulations that our advice is to say, as succinctly as possible, go to a specialist adviser who deals with Lloyd's underwriters.

Is there any special tax treatment for subcontractors?

The Construction Industry Scheme (CIS) works as follows:

1. There is a verification process which determines whether subcontractors should be paid gross or net. Subcontractors applying for registration have to prove their identity to HMRC, who then register the applicant for payment under deduction at the 20 per cent rate. Those registering for gross payment have to satisfy three further tests:

(a) **Turnover test:** HMRC will look at your business turnover from construction work for the 12 months before you apply for gross payment status. Ignoring VAT and the cost of materials, your construction turnover must be at least:

   • £30,000 if you are a sole trader;

   • £30,000 for each partner in a partnership, or at least £200,000 for the whole partnership;

   • £30,000 for each relevant person within the company, or at least £200,000 for the whole company.

A relevant person is a director and/or a shareholder where it is a 'close' company. A close company is one where there are five or fewer participators, or any number of participators if all of them are directors. A participator is (broadly) anyone who has share capital or voting rights in the company.

(b) **Compliance test:** You and any directors or partners in the business, or beneficial shareholders (where the company is controlled by five or fewer people) must have submitted all tax returns and paid all tax due on time in the 12 months before your application. If HMRC has asked for any information about your tax affairs in that period, you will need to have given it to them.

You are allowed a few lapses or late payments in the 12 months and HMRC will ignore any, or all, of the following failures:

   • three late submissions of the CIS contractor monthly return, including 'nil' returns – up to 28 days late;

- three late payments of CIS/PAYE deductions – up to 14 days late;

- one late payment of self-assessment tax – up to 28 days late;

- any employer's end of year return made late;

- any late payment of Corporation Tax – up to 28 days late, including where any shortfall in the payment has incurred an interest charge, but no penalty;

- any self-assessment return made late;

- any payment not made by the due date, where it is less than £100.

(c) **Business test:** You will need to show HMRC that your business carries out construction work – or provides labour for construction work – in the UK, and that it is run largely through a bank account.

2. Contractors have to make monthly returns and provide monthly statements of amounts paid. Contractors have 14 days to send in the returns and make payment (17 days if the payment is made electronically) and nil returns have to be submitted.

3. The contractor has to declare that it considers the subcontractor to be self-employed. This is always a difficult area and the questionnaire on pages 39–42 may be a useful starting point.

4. There is a 30 per cent rate of deduction which is to be used for those who are not registered.

Contractors would be well advised to have suitable software in place to cope with the monthly returns and paperwork. Penalties range from £100 up to £3,000.

Is there any special tax treatment for royalties?

If you are an author or composer by profession, then your receipts are taxed as part of your professional earnings and you are able to deduct more expenses than otherwise would be the case. In principle, you pay tax in the year in which the royalties are received, but there are rules for spreading royalty receipts over a number of years and, should you fall within this case, we strongly advise you to seek professional advice.

How do I get tax relief for losses in my business?

Trading losses may be:

1. relieved against income or gains of the same year;

2. relieved against income or gains of the previous year;

3. carried forward against future profits of the same trade.

In the case of both points 1 and 2, you must claim the full loss, up to the total income for that year. For individuals carrying on a trade in a non-active capacity, i.e. spending on average less than ten hours per week on the commercial activities of the trade, there is an annual limit of £25,000 for losses which can be set against other income in the year.

The amount of Income Tax relief that an individual may claim for deduction from their total income in a tax year is restricted. The limit is the greater of £50,000 or 25 per cent of the individual's adjusted total income.

Reliefs subject to the limit include:

• Trade loss relief against total income.

• Early trade losses relief.

• Post-cessation trade relief.

The limit does not apply to relief in the following circumstances:

• To deductions of trade loss relief, or post-cessation trade relief, made from profits of the same trade.

• To the extent that the trade loss relief is attributable to deductions of overlap relief.

Are there any special rules about claiming farm losses?

Because a number of wealthy people used to claim the substantial losses they made through their farming activities against their other substantial income, HMRC said that it would limit the number of years for which someone in this category could go on claiming farming losses.

How many years of farm losses can one utilise before having to carry forward those losses?

For a new farming business which is starting up, you can claim loss relief for six years. For an ongoing farming business, i.e. not a commencement scenario, the answer is five. A loss in the sixth tax year of a consecutive run of farming losses can only be relieved against later profits of the same trade. Once you have made a farming profit then the five-year sequence starts again.

The figure of loss or profit is arrived at before claiming capital allowances.

HMRC allows stud farms to incur losses for 11 years.

What are Class 4 National Insurance thresholds?

If you are trading and your profits exceed £8,060, you have to pay nine per cent Class 4 National Insurance contributions on the figure of your profits above £8,060 with an annual upper earnings limit of £43,000. Above this upper earnings limit, you have to pay two per cent on all profits above this figure.

What is a partnership?

A partnership is a formal business arrangement entered into by two or more people whereby the profits and losses of a business are shared in agreed proportions.

In order for HMRC to be happy that a partnership exists, it may want to see a number of the following items before it will agree to tax the business as a partnership:

- A partnership deed

- The names of partners on bank statements

- The names of partners on business letterheadings and other printed stationery

- Some sort of evidence that the parties agreed that there should be a formal partnership between them

There are restrictions on losses made by 'non-active' partners in the first four years. If the loss is claimed against other income or gains, it is restricted to the capital contribution made, unless the partner works more than ten hours a week for the partnership.

Should I go into partnership with my spouse/civil partner?

If your spouse or civil partner makes a genuine contribution to the business either by way of capital contribution or by way of time worked for it, then there is no reason why they should not become a partner. It is important for any partnership to be a real one (and not simply a tax dodge – because those don't work). Due recognition must be given to the fact that there are certain legal obligations which go with being a partner.

Obvious cases where husband and wife partnerships should exist are where they both share equally in the work and it's only right and proper that they should be partners. However, there are some disadvantages:

- both partners become jointly and severally liable for the partnership debts and this can put the family home at risk;

- in the case of divorce, the 'busting' of the partnership can result in the complete cessation of the business.

Where there is a bona fide husband/wife partnership, the following documentation should be available to prove to HMRC the existence of the partnership:

1. · There should be a letter issued to all customers of the business stating the appointment of a new partner and the date of the appointment.

2. There should be a written partnership agreement.

3. The names of the partners should appear on the letterheads and invoices, etc. of the business.

4. The names of the partners should appear on the business bank account.

5. The names of the partners should appear in the advertising and promotional literature.

6. If the business is VAT-registered, then it should be registered as a partnership with both the names of the partners on the VAT Return.

7. There should be a Notice of Particulars of Ownership displayed at the business's main centre so that any casual caller will see that there is a partnership in existence.

Do I need to have a partnership deed?

Our advice to any partners is that there should be a partnership deed so that, if anything should happen to one of the partners, or they should fall out, there is a legal agreement entered into at the start which establishes how the partnership should be dissolved and how the assets and liabilities should be allocated.

What are limited liability partnerships?

The Limited Liability Partnerships Act 2000 allows organisations the flexibility to enjoy limited liability while organising themselves (sharing profits, etc.) as partnerships. The limited liability partnership (LLP) is a separate legal entity. It's governed by an agreement between the members (the incorporation document). It is required to file at Companies House similar information to that required of companies, but it is taxed as a partnership.

We are ambivalent about LLPs because we regard the limitation of liability as being more theoretical than real. When companies fail, the directors often have to pay up on previously given personal guarantees and, if the company has failed through any negligence on the part of the directors, then they can be sued as private individuals. The same can apply to limited liability partners.

In principle, we think LLPs are a good thing, but in practice we don't think they have made much difference to anybody. Not that many LLPs have been registered and those that have are mainly large professional firms. There can be occasions when an LLP structure, rather than a limited company, is more suited to a new business; an example of this is when losses are expected to be made in the first year or two, and the partners have other income against which these losses can be relieved.

What happens if partners change?

Partnership changes are notified to HMRC by way of the Partnership Tax Return. When partners change, the apportionment of profits or losses is likely also to change. When the agreed profit or loss for the year in question is allocated to the varying partners (whether static, incoming or outgoing), that share is shown clearly on the Partnership Tax Return and the individual partners themselves pay the tax that their share attracts.

How are partnerships taxed?

Partnerships have their own Tax Return. The accounts are entered into the relevant boxes on the Partnership Tax Return and the profits or losses are allocated between the partners in the agreed proportions.

In addition, the partnership must prepare individual sheets called either 'Partnership (Short)' or 'Partnership (Long)' depending on the nature of the income that the partnership earns, and these individual sheets are handed to the partners themselves for attaching to their own individual personal Tax Returns.

In other words, partnerships don't pay tax. It's the partners who pay tax on their share of the profits or claim relief for their share of the losses.

What happens about partnership capital gains?

If a partnership makes a capital gain, the proceeds of sale are included on the Partnership Tax Return. The chargeable gain is computed and then each partner's share is added to his or her personal Tax Return, so that each pays Capital Gains Tax on his or her share of the gain.

How long do I have to keep my accounting records?

There is a legal requirement to keep accounting records for six years from the Tax Return filing deadline to which the accounts relate.

Why might HM Revenue & Customs inquire into my tax affairs?

HM Revenue & Customs (HMRC) is entitled to investigate for one of three reasons; either:

1. it thinks a minor point is wrong and needs to be corrected (an 'aspect' enquiry); or

2. it doesn't like the look of the accounts and suspects that there may be something fundamentally wrong (a 'full' enquiry); or

3. the nasty bit, a Tax Return may be selected at random. But few, if any, are so selected these days. HMRC's approach is risk based. Businesses

that handle a lot of cash are far more likely to be selected than those that do not.

3. HMRC is gathering a lot of data on an increasing range of different businesses. This will allow them to ascertain what the 'normal' gross profit rates are for a given type of business. Therefore, when a business submits account and the gross profit percentage is outside of HMRC's expected range, this could trigger an enquiry.

CHAPTER 7

Income from land and property

What is the wear-and-tear allowance?

This applied to furnished lettings only, but was abolished with effect from 6 April 2016. It's normal for taxpayers in receipt of income from land and property to claim all their allowable property expenses (see Appendix 5 for a template for identifying those expenses) against their rental income. However, instead of claiming for the cost of renewing furniture, furnishings and fixtures such as cookers, dishwashers or washing machines, taxpayers were entitled to charge a ten per cent wear-and-tear allowance instead. This ten per cent allowance is calculated as ten per cent of rent received less Council Tax and water rates paid (see below).

From 6 April 2016, relief can only be claimed for the actual expenditure incurred in replacing furnishings.

How do I claim losses from land and property?

There is a difference between the tax treatment of a land and property loss and a trading loss. Losses from land and property businesses can only be carried forward and set against profits in subsequent years from land and property. If you have land or property overseas, any losses made can only be relieved against future profits from that same property.

What is the difference between furnished lettings and furnished holiday lettings?

Furnished lettings

If you receive income from furnished lettings, it's taxed under the property income rules.

If you provide laundry, meals, domestic help, etc. for your tenants, then you may be able to claim that you are running a self-employed business – as you usually can if you are providing holiday lettings (see below). The advantage of running your property enterprise as a trading business means that there are usually more expenses you can claim against Income Tax and, in addition, you may be able to claim Entrepreneurs' Relief for Capital Gains Tax and business property relief for Inheritance Tax purposes. However, this does depend to a large extent on the amount of services you are providing.

Furnished holiday lettings

The definition of furnished holiday lettings is as follows:

- The accommodation must be available for holiday lets for at least 210 days per year.

- The accommodation must be commercially let for at least 105 days in the year.

- No let is to exceed 155 days.

There are special rules for the years of commencement and cessation. The income is treated as earned income (a trade) attracting Capital Gains Tax rollover relief and Entrepreneurs' Relief. Tax-saving ideas worth thinking about:

- Rollover of capital gains on the sale of trading assets into the purchase of holiday accommodation.

- Any gain on the sale of the holiday accommodation may eventually attract Capital Gains Tax at only ten per cent. (See page 111.)

- You can claim capital allowances on furniture and equipment.

However:

- If you buy the accommodation with a substantial mortgage, HM Revenue & Customs (HMRC) may regard your motives as not being commercial.

- Don't forget about the VAT consequences, if you are VAT-registered.

- Any losses that are incurred can only be carried forward and set against profits of the same holiday business, not other categories of income or lettings. Furnished holiday lettings within the UK, compared to any outside the UK but in the European Economic Area, say in France, are also separated for loss purposes.

What is rent-a-room relief?

From 6 April 2016, if you let a room in your house and you are an owner-occupier, or a tenant who is subletting, the first £7,500 of any income is tax free, i.e. a rent of £144.23 per week is tax free. (This figure used to be £4,250 per annum.) If the rent is higher than £7,500, you either elect to pay tax on the surplus above £7,500 (without relief for expenses) or you can treat the arrangement as being a furnished letting and prepare accounts.

This relief is available whether you rent out just one room to a lodger or you run a bed & breakfast business from your house. Relief is not normally available to people living abroad or in job-related accommodation and letting their home while they are away.

Woodlands – what are the rules about selling timber?

There is no Income Tax charge on woodlands; neither woodland rent nor the sale of timber is taxed. There is no charge to Capital Gains Tax on trees that are standing or felled. In other words, profits on the sale of timber are not taxed at all and losses are not allowable.

How are property developers taxed?

You may find, perhaps because you are a developer, that you carry out a number of purchases and sales of land and buildings and that, instead of these transactions being treated as falling within the Capital Gains Tax regime, the profits and losses you make are caught under the Income Tax regime. There are some taxpayers who have been badly caught by this and in principle it's quite difficult to give a hard-and-fast rule as to when somebody moves from the Capital Gains Tax regime to the Income Tax regime. However, all may not be lost, because when a capital asset falls within the Income Tax regime, not only are the losses more favourably treated, but also there are usually more expenses that can be claimed as well.

In our opinion, you should seek professional advice if this eventuality comes to pass in your case.

What are the tax rules for buy-to-let investors?

There is an interesting addition to HMRC's manuals which indicates that interest on funds borrowed for private purposes may be deductible against rental income in certain circumstances. This has wide-reaching implications for buy-to-let investors.

One example in the manual covers Mr A who owns a flat in London and is moving abroad. He decides to let the property while he is away. During his period of ownership, the property has trebled in value. He renegotiates the mortgage to convert it to a buy-to-let mortgage and borrows a further amount which he uses to buy a property overseas. Can he claim tax relief on the interest against the rents? Well, HMRC says that owners of businesses (and renting property is a business for tax purposes) are entitled to withdraw their capital from the business, even though substitute funding then has to be provided by interest-bearing loans. In the case of Mr A, his opening balance sheet shows the following:

Original mortgage	80,000	Property at market value	375,000
Capital account	295,000		
	£375,000		£375,000

When Mr A renegotiates his mortgage, he borrows a further £125,000 which goes through his property business. He then withdraws this amount to fund the purchase of the property overseas. By the end of the first year of letting, his balance sheet shows the following.

Mortgage	205,000	Property at market value	375,000
Capital account b/f	295,000		
Less drawings	(125,000)		
Carry forward	170,000		
	£375,000		£375,000

Although he has withdrawn capital from the business, the interest on the mortgage loan is allowable in full because it's funding the transfer of the property to the business at its open market value at the time the business started. Although HMRC's example has a further mortgage of £125,000, it seems that Mr A could withdraw a further £170,000 of tax-allowable finance. However, he should not take out more than he puts in as his capital account will be in the red (i.e. overdrawn).

The best advice is not to assume that you will automatically get tax relief and to take professional advice remortgaging. However, this seemingly good news pales into insignificance when viewing the changes that are coming into force from April 2017. Even though this book is concerned primarily with the 2016/17 tax year, see 'What are the new rules being introduced for buy-to-let landlords?' on page 96, on this potentially devastating change.

What are the new rules being introduced for buy-to-let landlords?

A major change is being introduced in the way that landlords claim relief for mortgage interest against their rental income. Historically, the amount of interest paid has been claimed as an expense against the rental income; the consequence of this being that if a landlord was a higher rate taxpayer, he in effect got tax relief on the loan interest at 40 per cent.

From 6 April 2017, higher rate relief for loan interest is being phased out as follows:

- In 2017 to 2018, the deduction from property income (as is currently allowed) will be restricted to 75 per cent of finance costs, with the remaining 25 per cent being available as a basic rate tax reduction.

- In 2018 to 2019, 50 per cent finance costs deduction and 50 per cent given as a basic rate tax reduction.

- In 2019 to 2020, 25 per cent finance costs deduction and 75 per cent given as a basic rate tax reduction.

- From 2020 to 2021, all financing costs incurred by a landlord will be given as a basic rate tax reduction.

Please note that if you are only liable to tax on your rental profits at the basic rate, this will not affect you.

To facilitate this change, the way in which the relief is given is changing. See the example below to illustrate how things will be transformed.

Picture the scenario where rental income is £8,000 per annum and mortgage interest in the year is £6,000, and there are no other expenses. The landlord has employment income of £50,000 in the year and is therefore liable to tax at 40 per cent.

In the 2016/17 tax year there would be a profit of £2,000 which would create a tax liability of £800. The landlord's net position would be rent of £8,000, less interest of £6,000, less tax due of £800, which leaves him with £1,200 in his pocket.

In the 2020/21 tax year, the liability is first calculated ignoring loan interest and so the first part of the calculation is to charge 40 per cent tax on the rental income which comes to £3,200. The second stage of the calculation gives loan interest relief at 20 per cent which comes to £1,200.

Therefore the landlord has had rental income of £8,000, has paid out £6,000 in loan interest and also has a tax liability of £2,000 (£3,200 - £1,200) leaving him with zero net income.

Most landlords will have other expenses as well as the loan interest and so it can be seen how a once profitable property business can become loss-making. This is why this matter is so very important to those who have buy-to-let properties. The changes are being phased in over four years, but we fear this will still hit a lot of people very hard.

If you are currently a higher rate taxpayer, or you anticipate being so in the next few years, this issue is of great importance to you and you must consider your options carefully. The Chancellor has announced that large property businesses, and landlords who own their letting properties in a company, will not be affected by this change, i.e. they will still be able to claim the full amount of loan interest relief. However, the question of whether or not you can or should transfer your buy-to-let properties into a company is one which requires careful consideration and we recommend that you consult an accountant on this issue.

What is the difference between joint tenants and tenants in common?

While it may seem strange to refer to property owners as being tenants, those owning it as joint tenants own the property in equal shares. Those owning it as tenants in common own it in a nominated or chosen proportion which need not be equal.

One consequence of owning property as joint tenants is that on the death of one, his share passes automatically to the survivor. If the property is owned as tenants in common, on death the share doesn't pass automatically to the other owner.

How are lease premiums taxed?

Lease premiums are now becoming 'more a thing of the past', but if you do grant a lease of not more than 50 years' duration, for which you receive a premium, then you will be assessed for Income Tax on the premium. The taxable amount is quite complicated to calculate but (putting a block of ice on your head we will try to explain it): you take the premium and reduce it by 1/50 of its amount for each complete period of 12 months, other than the first 12 months, and this amount is subject to Income Tax. The balance of the premium is normally subject to Capital Gains Tax.

What are the rules for leases and Stamp Duty?

These are complicated so you should seek professional advice. In effect, if you take out a lease you are likely to have to pay Stamp Duty Land Tax (see page 160 for more information).

What is the Annual Tax on Enveloped Dwellings?

In general terms, this is an annual tax charge which arises on a company which owns residential property in the UK, valued at more than £500,000. There are a number of exemptions from the charge, a common one being that the property is rented out. The table below sets out the annual charges that are due.

Annual Tax on Enveloped Dwelling (ATED) returns are due by 30 April of the tax year in question, and a return has to be submitted to HMRC even if full relief is available from the charge.

Property value	Annual charge
£500,000 - £1,000,000	£3,500
£1,000,000 - £2,000,000	£7,000
£2,000,000 - £5,000,000	£23,350
£5,000,000 - £10,000,000	£54,450
£10,000,000 - £20,000,000	£109,050
More than £20,000,000	£218,200

CHAPTER 8

Income from dividends and interest

What are the new rules on dividend taxation?

From 6 April 2016, the dividend tax credit has been abolished, which means that from this point forwards dividends are in effect paid gross. From this date, the government has introduced the Dividend Tax Allowance; this is an allowance of up to £5,000 per annum within which all dividends received are free of tax.

If you receive more than £5,000 of dividends in the 2016/17 tax year, and your total income is within the basic rate band, i.e. not exceeding £43,000, then tax is charged at 7.5 per cent on the dividends which exceed this tax free allowance. Do be aware, however, that the £5,000 tax free allowance forms part of your basic rate band, therefore your income including the tax free dividends must not exceed £43,000.

If you are a higher rate taxpayer (income between £43,000 and £150,000), then the dividends in excess of £5,000 are taxed at 32.5 per cent.

If you are an additional rate taxpayer (income in excess of £150,000) then your dividend income in excess of £5,000 is taxed at 38.1 per cent.

What are the new rules on interest I receive?

From 6 April 2016, banks, building societies and similar institutions will no longer deduct any tax from the interest that you are paid. Therefore, everyone will receive untaxed interest; from the same date, the Personal Savings Allowance is introduced. This exempts from tax the first £1,000 of interest received by basic rate taxpayers in the year. (Those with total adjusted net income of less than £43,000.)

Higher rate taxpayers (those with total adjusted net income in excess of £43,000) are eligible for only £500 of Personal Savings Allowance.

Those with total adjusted net incomes in excess of £150,000 are not eligible for any Personal Savings Allowance.

The term 'interest' also includes interest distributions from unit trusts, OEICs and investment trusts, income from government or company bonds, and most types of Purchased Life Annuity payments.

Interest received on ISAs are not included as this is already tax free.

What is the tax position on bank interest?

Following on from the previous point, if you receive interest which is in excess of your Personal Savings Allowance, then you will owe tax on this. If HMRC are aware of this then your 2016/17 tax code may already have been adjusted to collect the additional tax that is due. If this is not the case, then you need to inform HMRC of the position so that you can pay the correct amount of tax.

Does HMRC know what interest I have received?

HMRC have access to tremendous amounts of data already, and this is increasing all the time. It is anticipated that HMRC will be informed of the amounts of bank and building society interest that you receive each year. Therefore, in theory, they should have the correct data for you. However, it is always prudent to check the figures that HMRC quote, to ensure they they do indeed have the correct details for you.

What is the tax position on annuities?

Annuities are sources of income usually enjoyed by the elderly. The individual makes an investment in the annuity and over the remaining period of his life receives payments in connection with this annuity, some of which is capital and some of which is taxable income. When the annuity is paid it will be clearly shown how much is capital (and this is not taxable), how much is income and how much tax has been deducted. You should total the income elements of each payment and enter the gross totals together with the tax deducted on your Tax Return.

What are ISAs?

ISA stands for Individual Savings Account. They are free from Income and Capital Gains Tax. Following recent changes in government legislation, future ISA limits are now tied to the Retail Prices Index (RPI). However, the Chancellor still has the power to make arbitrary changes to the limits allowed.

For the 2015/16 and 2016/17 tax years, the overall ISA limit is £15,240, all of which can be held in cash.

Junior ISAs are aimed at children and have different limits; for the 2015/16 and 2016/17 tax years, the limit is £4,080.

From 6 April 2016, ISAs have been made more flexible: money can be withdrawn and replaced within the same tax year without the replacement money counting towards the annual ISA limit. This policy also covers cash held in a stock-and-shares ISA.

What is the Help to Buy ISA?

In the 2015 Budget, it was announced that from the Autumn of 2015 a new type of ISA would be introduced, available from banks and building societies. The accounts will only be available for four years, but once an account is opened, you can keep saving for as long as you like.

The account can be opened with a lump sum of up to £1,000, but thereafter you are limited to saving a maximum of £200 per month. When you come to buy your first UK property, the government will give you a bonus up to a maximum of £3,000, depending on how much you have saved. (Basically, it is a £50 bonus for every £200 saved.) Therefore, savings of £12,000 would be boosted to £15,000 by the bonus. The accounts are limited to one per person, therefore two people buying a property together could have an account each.

The bonus is only available for home purchases of up to £450,000 in London and £250,000 elsewhere in the country.

What are Venture Capital Trusts?

Venture Capital Trusts were introduced to encourage individuals to invest indirectly in unquoted trading companies. If you do this, you will be exempt from Income Tax on dividends and Capital Gains Tax on sales of shares acquired of up to £200,000 a year. In addition, Income Tax relief of 30 per cent applies on up to £200,000 in any tax year, if you subscribe for new shares which you then hold for at least five years.

What is the Enterprise Investment Scheme?

The Enterprise Investment Scheme (EIS) was introduced to encourage individuals to invest directly in unquoted trading companies. There are various rules governing how this is organised. If you make an EIS investment, you will be exempt from tax on capital gains (but not dividends) arising from shares acquired of up to £1 million a year. Also, if you subscribe for new shares which you then hold for at least three years, there is Income Tax relief based on 30 per cent of up to £1 million of that EIS investment in any tax year.

It's also possible to defer Capital Gains Tax on the gain arising on the sale of any asset by reducing that gain by the amount of EIS investment. The tax becomes payable when the EIS shares are sold.

What is the Seed Enterprise Investment Scheme?

The Seed Enterprise Investment Scheme (SEIS) is similar to the EIS, but it's aimed specifically at investments in small start-up businesses and has different rules. The company should be carrying on a qualifying trade, generally outside of finance or investment, have fewer than 25 employees, and have assets of less than £200,000. The subscriber can invest up to £100,000 in a single tax year, with an overall maximum investment in each company of £150,000.

The investor must own less than 30 per cent of the business and it must be a UK company. The best bit is that 50 per cent tax relief is given on the investment regardless of the investor's marginal rate of tax. Like EIS investments, SEIS investments are free from Capital Gains Tax when sold, provided they have been held for at least three years. Any taxpayer who has a Capital Gains Tax liability will receive 50 per cent CGT relief when they reinvest those gains into seed companies.

What are REITs?

A REIT is a Real Estate Investment Trust, a special type of investment trust designed to encourage investment in the property sector. It enables investors to invest in the property market without buying a property and provides tax breaks for property companies by exempting income and gains from tax.

Income paid to investors will be net of basic rate tax. So, if you receive a payment of £80, the gross figure you should put on your Tax Return is £100 from which tax at 20 per cent has been deducted and, if you are a basic rate taxpayer, no further tax is due. If you are liable to tax at 40 or 45 per cent, you will have to pay the extra 20 or 25 per cent under self-assessment. These payments are known as PIDs (Property Income Distributions). Just to make things confusing, some REITs will also pay dividends which come with a ten per cent tax credit (see the first section of this chapter). The voucher that accompanies the payment should make it clear whether the payment is a PID or a dividend.

CHAPTER 9

Life assurance policies

What do I need to know about the taxation of life assurance?

The answer to this is probably 'not very much'. Life assurance used to enjoy a highly favoured tax status, but since 1984 this has been reduced. Some benefits remain and the overall concept is dealt with below.

There are three main types of life assurance. Firstly, there is term assurance, the sum of which is only paid if you die during the term of the policy; there is no savings element in this policy, but they tend to be cheap. Secondly, there is whole of life assurance, whereby the sum is payable on your death at any time. Thirdly, there is an endowment policy, where the amount assured is payable on your death within the term of the policy or at the policy's end.

If you invest now in a life assurance policy (normally called 'Single Premium Bonds'), you will pay no basic rate Income Tax when you draw the money out from it. However, you may be liable to the balance between the higher rates of tax and the basic rate tax if certain circumstances apply.

If what follows sounds complicated, don't worry, because the life assurance company is bound to send not only you, but also HM Revenue & Customs (HMRC) a certificate detailing the information about your policy and the gain that you have made.

In principle, if you withdraw no more than five per cent of your investment each year, there will be no further tax implications on this sort of policy. If you withdraw more than five per cent, there may be tax to pay, but we do suggest that rather than going into complicated calculations, you should take advice from either HMRC or a qualified accountant.

What are chargeable events?

A chargeable event is when you withdraw money from a life assurance policy or bond. As you will see from the previous question, unless you withdraw more than five per cent of your investment in any tax year, there will be no tax implications. Indeed, even if you do withdraw more than five per cent, if you are a basic rate taxpayer, with the aid of top slicing relief there may not be any additional tax liability arising.

What are bonds?

There are all sorts of bonds, including Euro Bonds, Guaranteed Income Bonds and Single Premium Bonds. The subject of Euro Bonds doesn't really fall into the scope of this book, but in the case of Guaranteed Income Bonds these resemble annuities and only the income element is subject to Income Tax.

In the case of chargeable income bonds, we refer you to the question above relating to the taxation of life assurance, where we hope you will find the answer.

What is 'top slicing relief'?

Top slicing relief is complicated and we do suggest that, if you want a full answer which you will properly understand, you either attend the local Tax Office or refer to a professional adviser. Basically, it's a relief available to individuals (but not to companies) against what otherwise would be a higher rate of tax on any investment gain you might make on the surrender or sale of a life assurance policy.

What are 'partial surrenders'?

If you make a partial surrender of a life assurance policy, and this is usually the case when you receive annual payments from a Single Premium Bond, it may give rise to tax but only if you withdraw more than five per cent of your original investment.

As with areas of this chapter on life assurance policies, we recommend you take professional advice, because the explanation of this complicated area of the tax law is beyond the ambit of this book.

Can I claim tax relief on my permanent health insurance payments?

Permanent health insurance policies are intended to provide you with an income should illness prevent you from working. If your employer pays the premium on your policy, it will obtain a tax allowance on the payment it makes and you will have to pay tax on any benefit that you receive.

If you make the payments yourself, whether as an employee or as a self-employed person, you won't obtain any tax relief, but any benefits paid to you under these circumstances will be tax free.

What are 'purchased life annuities'?

Purchased life annuities are investments normally taken out by the elderly which receive favourable tax treatment, but do contain substantial risk.

The basic principle is that you invest a lump sum with an insurance company; then each year, up until the day of your death, it will repay part of the capital together with interest. The interest is taxed but the capital is not. This is one way of increasing the spendable income of elderly people. However, the danger is that if an annuity is taken out on day one and the annuitant dies on day two, all the money is lost.

CHAPTER 10

Capital Gains Tax

What is Capital Gains Tax?

If you make a gain on the disposal of any investments, land and buildings, jewellery, antiques or any form of other property, you may be liable to Capital Gains Tax on the gain. The main activities that we, as accountants, see our clients paying Capital Gains Tax on are as follows:

- Sale of businesses
- Sale of stocks and shares
- Sale of antiques over £6,000
- Sale of property
- Gifts of any of the above

Here are some of the assets that are exempt from the Capital Gains Tax net:

- Private motor vehicles
- Your own home (but not including a second home)
- National Savings Certificates
- Foreign currency
- Decorations for gallantry (unless purchased)
- Betting winnings (including pools, lotteries and Premium Bonds)
- Compensation or damages for any wrong or injury suffered
- British government securities

- Life assurance policies and annuities
- Chattels (i.e. movable possessions) sold for £6,000 or less
- Assets given to a charity or the nation
- Enterprise and Seed Investment Scheme shares held for three years
- Timber and uncut trees
- Individual Savings Accounts
- Venture Capital Trust shares held for five years
- Guns, wine, antiques – providing they are not used in a business
- Debts
- Qualifying Corporate Bonds
- Child Trust Funds
- Cashbacks

A rough guide to Capital Gains Tax is provided at Appendix 6.

How does Capital Gains Tax work?

For individuals, the rate of Capital Gains Tax (CGT) for non-property gains is 10 per cent for standard rate taxpayers and 20 per cent for higher rate taxpayers. This is charged on all gains above the annual exempt amount, which is £11,100. The gain is treated as the top slice of income in order to determine whether it is chargeable wholly at 10 per cent or at a combination of 10 per cent up to the basic rate band limit and then 20 per cent on the remainder. The historical 18 per cent and 28 per cent rates will continue to apply in a similar manner to disposals of residential property which do not qualify for Private Residence Relief. The chargeable gain is the difference between the sale proceeds (less costs of sale) and original cost or market value at 31 March 1982 if later, plus any improvement costs incurred in the intervening period. If the disposal was by way of gift, then you use market value as the disposal 'proceeds'. Capital losses may be deducted from capital gains or, if these are insufficient, carried forward to subsequent years.

The chargeable gains of companies are included in their total taxable profits for the relevant period. They are calculated as for individuals with one exception: companies may claim an Indexation Allowance to take account of inflation. The Retail Prices Index – from March 1982 onwards – is applied to the period of ownership of the asset to calculate this.

What is Entrepreneurs' Relief?

Entrepreneurs' Relief gives preferential treatment to the disposal of business assets. This term includes a trading business carried on either alone or in partnership, assets of that business, shares in the individual's own trading company and assets owned by the individual but used in his trading company or business. Furnished holiday letting properties are also regarded as business assets, but not properties used for any other type of letting. Qualifying gains are taxed at a rate of 10 per cent.

There is a lifetime limit of £10 million upon which the Entrepreneurs' Relief can be claimed and claims can be made on more than one occasion to utilise the lifetime limit. The business must have been owned for at least one year ending on the date of the disposal. If you are selling a property that was used in the business, then you have to sell it within three years of selling the business or you will lose the relief on it.

Who pays Capital Gains Tax?

The quick answer is: the person making the gain; but where an asset is given away and the taxpayer may think that he has made no gain (because no money has been received) and therefore has no tax to pay, he may easily be mistaken. Because a gift constitutes a disposal, if there is a gain on that disposal, even the giver, who is in receipt of no disposal proceeds, pays Capital Gains Tax on the gain that he is deemed to have made on the disposal.

In general, to pay Capital Gains Tax (CGT) one has to be a UK-resident taxpayer, which includes a company, trust or partnership. However, from 6 April 2015, even non-residents have now become liable to capital gains made on the disposal of residential property. However, if you are resident but not domiciled in this country, you are only charged Capital Gains Tax on your overseas realisations of assets when you bring the money here.

Is there an annual exemption from CGT?

Every year, there is an annual exemption from Capital Gains Tax. In the year 2016/17, your first £11,100 of gains is exempt. In the case of trusts, it's £5,550. The rate of Capital Gains Tax (CGT) is 28 per cent for trusts.

What can I set against my CGT liability?

Apart from the annual exemption, you can set the costs of acquisition of the asset, including purchase price, and the sale costs, against the gain.

In addition, if you bought an asset on which you have incurred enhancement or improvement expenditure, then that too will be allowed as a cost. Certain costs such as accountant's fees are not allowed, but if you are looking for allowable costs, and because this subject can be so wide-ranging, we suggest you talk either to a professional accountant or to HM Revenue & Customs (HMRC).

Can I get any relief for capital losses?

If you sell or give away a capital asset at a loss, it's normally deductible from any capital gains that you have made during the same year and any remaining unrelieved losses are available to carry forward against future capital gains. If you give or sell an asset to a 'connected person' (generally a blood relative or a business partner/fellow director), the loss can only be used against gains on assets sold to the same party.

However, there is some relief available from a different quarter. If you make a trading loss in your business and don't have enough income to cover it, you can elect for the unused losses from that trading period to be set against your capital gains for that same tax year or for the previous tax year. In other words, capital gains can be reduced by trading losses. Again, we would suggest that you seek professional advice on this.

There is also scope to claim relief for capital losses arising on qualifying shares which have been subscribed for, against your general income either in the year of the loss or the previous tax year. Shares are qualifying shares if EIS relief is attributable to them, or where this is not the case, they are shares in a qualifying trading company which have been subscribed for by the individual.

How and when is Capital Gains Tax paid?

Capital Gains Tax is payable by individuals on 31 January following the end of the tax year in which the gain was made. It's payable by companies, along with the rest of their Corporation Tax, nine months after their year end.

What are the rules for part-disposals?

Where part of an asset is disposed of, you have to work out the cost applicable to the part sold. The rules are complicated. A special rule applies to small part-disposals of land and, provided that the sale proceeds don't exceed either £20,000 or one fifth of the total market value of the land, you may deduct the sale proceeds from your base cost rather than pay any tax now.

What are the rules for private residences and Capital Gains Tax relief?

Normally, the house or flat in which you live is exempt from Capital Gains Tax when you sell it. The property must have been your only or main residence during the period of ownership. During the last 18 months of ownership, the property is always regarded as your main residence even if you don't live there. You can also be absent for periods totalling three years and for any period throughout which you worked abroad. To qualify for these additional periods of exemption, you must live in the property both before and after the absence. In addition, if you had any work which required you to live in job-related accommodation, that also doesn't stand against you for Capital Gains Tax purposes. Any periods of absence in excess of the periods allowed result in the relevant proportion of your sale profit being charged to Capital Gains Tax.

You can also get relief for any period when your house was let up to a maximum of £40,000 (or the amount of Private Residence Relief whichever is the least per owner).

If a specific part of your house is set aside for business purposes, then that proportion of your profits on the sale of the house will be taxable. However, if you don't have any rooms used **exclusively** for business purposes you won't normally be liable to any Capital Gains Tax if you sell your house.

Special consideration needs to be given to houses with a lot of land alongside them. If land is sold in excess of what HMRC regards to be a normal area of garden in character for the house that is being sold, then the gain on the sale of such extra land will be subject to Capital Gains Tax.

Within two years of buying a second property, you should send in a letter (called an 'election') in which you disclose to the taxman which of your two properties you are treating as your private residence for Capital Gains Tax purposes. Otherwise, the taxman will decide for you and the decision will be based on the facts (i.e. where you have actually spent the majority of your time).

What are the rules for chattels sold for less than £6,000?

A chattel is an asset which is 'tangible movable property', such as a work of art or a set of chairs. Provided that the asset fetches no more than £6,000, HMRC doesn't require you to pay Capital Gains Tax on it. However, if you have a set of dining room chairs and each one is not worth £6,000 but in total the set is worth say £30,000, the set will attract Capital Gains Tax on it, because a set is treated as one chattel.

What Capital Gains Tax relief is there for the sale of business assets?

In principle, you are liable to Capital Gains Tax in respect of the sale of any assets used in your business. However, if all of the sale proceeds are invested in further business assets that are purchased within one year before or three years after the sale, you can claim Rollover Relief as a result of which the gain on the disposal is rolled over into the cost of the new business assets acquired. Therefore, no tax is paid until the new business assets are sold, unless they too are replaced.

For these assets to qualify they must be either land and buildings, fixed plant and machinery, goodwill, milk and potato quota or other agricultural quotas including payment entitlements under the Single Payment Scheme. Please note that motor vehicles don't qualify.

What Capital Gains Tax relief is there for gifts?

In principle, gifts of assets don't escape Capital Gains Tax, but gifts of the following attract a special relief called holdover relief:

- Business assets
- Agricultural property
- Shares and securities in a family trading company
- A gift which gives rise to an immediate charge to Inheritance Tax

Holdover relief works in the same way as Rollover Relief. The gain is held over until such time as the recipient of the gift sells it.

Gifts which attract Inheritance Tax are rare, but one such example is when you transfer assets into a discretionary trust. Gifts to individuals and to trusts for disabled people, are classed as potentially exempt transfers (PETs) and Inheritance Tax won't be payable, unless you die within seven years of making the gift. However, tapering relief may reduce the Inheritance Tax payable after three years.

What are the aspects of CGT if I live abroad?

If you are resident in this country (see page 136 for further information on these terms), you are liable to tax on any capital gains realised anywhere in the world. However, if you have realised a gain in a country which won't allow the proceeds to be sent to the UK, you can claim for the gain to be deferred until the year in which you receive the money in this country.

If you are non-resident in this country but are carrying on a trade in the UK, you are liable to CGT on the assets used in the business. If you are UK-domiciled, HMRC does have new powers to apportion certain capital gains of overseas trusts of which you are a beneficiary and this has caught out a number of wealthy people who transferred their assets abroad.

If you have left the UK for tax residence abroad, from 5 April 2015 you will be liable to CGT on gains made when selling UK residential property. You will be liable on the gain which relates to the period after 5 April 2015. Therefore, you will either need to know the value of your property at 5 April 2015, or you can use a straight-line time apportionment over the entire period of ownership. This is a complicated matter and professional advice should be sought. When obtaining property valuations, we would recommend at least two separate professional valuations, as this will reduce the risk of HMRC successfully arguing with your figures.

Generally speaking, if you are absent from the UK for at least five complete tax years, any other (non-residential) gains will be free from UK CGT.

Can I sell shares one day, creating enough gains to use up the annual Capital Gains Tax allowance, and buy them back the next day?

If you sell shares and buy them back within 30 days (known as the 30-day rule), for CGT purposes the disposal of the shares is matched against the purchase cost of the shares acquired within 30 days of the sale, not against the original acquisition cost. However, you can get around this problem if your spouse buys the shares back on the open market, and not directly from you.

Is there anything I can do to defer or avoid CGT?

Providing certain conditions are met, if you invest disposal proceeds into an Enterprise Investment Scheme (EIS) which would otherwise be liable to CGT, the gain on your investment can be deferred. Providing all qualifying conditions are met, the gain on the disposal of the EIS investment can be free of any CGT liability.

It is also possible to make an investment into a Seed Enterprise Investment Scheme (SEIS) company of sale proceeds, subject to CGT. There is a maximum investment of £100,000 but the reinvestment of £100,000 would permit the gain chargeable to be reduced by £50,000. Any gain made on the SEIS investment will be free of CGT, providing the qualifying conditions are met.

So, there are ways of reducing chargeable gains, but we strongly recommend that professional financial advice be taken by anyone considering making EIS and SEIS investments. Risks and conditions are attached to these investments, which must be clearly understood in order to gain the best taxation outcome. Investments of this sort are not suitable to everyone.

CHAPTER 11

Trusts and estates

What is a trust?

A trust is brought into existence when a person (called the 'settlor') transfers some of his assets to trustees (who become the legal owners) for the benefit of third parties, called 'beneficiaries' (the beneficial owners). A trust is a legal entity in itself. Another word for a trust is a settlement. Sometimes trusts are created under a Will and sometimes they are created during the lifetime of the settlor. Sometimes trusts are created to save tax, sometimes to protect assets; there are many and various reasons for setting up a trust.

Do the trustees have to complete a Tax Return and what tax do they pay?

Trustees do have to complete a Tax Return reporting their income and capital gains on an annual basis, although this is often prepared by an accountant. In cases where the beneficiaries have a life interest in the income of the trust (known as interest in possession trusts), the appropriate lower rate of tax is paid by the trustees and the beneficiaries are treated as having paid the tax that has been deducted by the trustees.

In the case of discretionary trusts (and again we are verging into the area where professional advice should be sought) sufficient extra tax must be paid to bring the total tax up to the rate applicable to trusts which is 45 per cent (38.1 per cent for dividends).

The trustees must pay the tax on 31 January and 31 July each year.

How are trusts in Wills affected by tax?

The main tax that affects Wills, triggered by the death of the person, is Inheritance Tax and there is a separate section in this book dealing with this very aspect. However, when someone dies his personal representative (PR) or executor will make sure that a personal Tax Return is completed from the start of the tax year to the date of the deceased's death. From the date of his death to the end of the tax year the PR will have to account for tax and report to the beneficiaries on the tax that the PR has deducted. Each year the PR will have to submit a Trust and Estate Tax Return to HM Revenue & Customs (HMRC). However, in the year in which the estate is wound up and all the assets have been distributed, the PR will only have to account for the tax on the income up to the date of distribution. In practice, if probate value is less than £2.5 million and the total tax due by the PR is less than £10,000, HMRC will accept a single computation and one-off payment.

What were accumulation and maintenance settlements (A&M trusts)?

An accumulation and maintenance trust was a form of discretionary trust created for the benefit of a minor, where the income from the trust was accumulated and not attributed to the beneficiaries until he reached the age of at least 18. The trustees were able to use the income of the trust to 'maintain' the beneficiaries; for example, to pay their school fees. These trusts used to have substantial Inheritance Tax advantages but have now been abolished.

What are discretionary trusts?

A discretionary trust is one in which the settlor gives discretion to the trustees as to how they treat the income and capital and to whom they distribute it. These trusts also pay Income Tax at the rate applicable to trusts of 45 per cent (and 38.1 per cent on dividends).

How do discretionary trusts pay Inheritance Tax?

A discretionary trust doesn't pay Inheritance Tax on a death, but it does pay Inheritance Tax on every tenth anniversary of the date of settlement if this was after 31 March 1983. The charge, called 'the periodic charge', is at 30 per cent of the lifetime rate, which is itself half of the rate on death. In principle, the rate of tax is therefore six per cent (i.e. 30 per cent of 20 per cent) of the assets in the trust, but the calculation is not an easy one and you should seek professional advice.

A discretionary trust also pays Inheritance Tax when any of the settled property leaves the trust. This is called an 'exit charge'. The rate of tax is determined by the length of time that has elapsed either since the creation of the trust or since the last periodic charge.

How do trusts pay Capital Gains Tax?

Most trusts attract half the annual exemption that is available for individuals. This is currently half of £11,100, i.e. £5,550 (for 2016/2017). The capital gains are worked out in accordance with the usual Capital Gains Tax rules (see chapter 10) and the tax on any capital gain is paid over at the same time as the balancing payment for the Income Tax, in other words 31 January following the end of the tax year. Trusts pay Capital Gains Tax at the rate of 28 per cent.

Trust modernisation

In 2003, the Chancellor announced plans to simplify and modernise the tax system for trusts. Initially, he began with these two:

1. Since 6 April 2005 discretionary trusts and accumulation and maintenance trusts have a standard rate band of £1,000. What this means in practice is that the first £1,000 of income is charged at either 7.5 per cent or 20 per cent, depending on the type of income. Income in excess of £1,000 will be taxed at 38.1 per cent or 45 per cent.

2. Since 6 April 2004 certain trusts with vulnerable beneficiaries are able to elect that the trust income and gains is taxed at the beneficiaries' tax rate if this proves more beneficial.

In his 2006 Budget he introduced the following series of measures against trusts.

1. Since 22 March 2006 gifts to either accumulation and maintenance settlements or interest in possession settlements (whether new or existing trusts) are regarded as chargeable transfers for Inheritance Tax purposes. This means that transfers into them above the nil-rate band are subject to tax at 20 per cent.

   New A&M trusts are subject to the ten-year charge of six per cent and, like discretionary trusts, there is also an exit charge from such trusts.

   These new charges do not apply to trusts for the disabled. Nor do they apply to a trust set up in a parent's Will for a minor child, so long as he is fully entitled to the assets at the age of 18.

   In other words, broadly speaking, the regime that used to apply to discretionary trusts now applies to A&M trusts as well.

2. Since 6 April 2008, existing accumulation and maintenance trusts are also caught by these rules, unless they have revised their trust deed to allow the beneficiary to receive the funds by the age of 18.

3. It was generally felt by the accountancy and legal profession that making significant sums available at the age of 18 was unwise. As a result of representations, the government only made one small concession. A new type of trust has been created, known as an age 18

to 25 trust. With such trusts, the beneficiary doesn't have to take capital at the age of 18, but must do so by the age of 25. For these trusts, there is no exit or ten-year charge while the beneficiary is under the age of 18. From 18 to 25 a reduced Inheritance Tax charge applies. The maximum payable is 4.2 per cent (instead of six per cent). Some parents may feel that paying tax at 4.2 per cent maximum is a better option than handing over a large capital sum to an 18 year old.

4. Since 22 March 2006, when an interest in possession trust comes to an end so that the property remains on trust, this is treated as the creation of new settled property. There is an immediate entry charge.

CHAPTER 12

Corporation Tax

What is Corporation Tax?

Corporation Tax is the tax that limited companies and unincorporated associations (such as clubs) pay on their profits. It's a tax on the profits of the company; profits include trading profits, rental income, interest and capital gains.

How is Corporation Tax assessed and paid?

Corporation Tax is accounted for in 12-month periods, unless the accounting period from its commencement to the first accounting date, or the last period of operation, is less than 12 months. (You may already be thinking that it's time to consult a professional accountant and, in our view, if you have a limited company and you are dealing with Corporation Tax you should certainly seek professional advice.)

Every company has to fill in an annual Corporation Tax Return (Form CT600) and this Return has to be submitted by the company secretary or the directors within 12 months of the end of the accounting period. However, tax has to be paid, assuming we are dealing with a small company, nine months after the end of the accounting period. Big companies have to pay Corporation Tax at more frequent intervals.

What is Corporation Tax self-assessment?

Corporation Tax self-assessment means that companies have to work out their Corporation Tax liability themselves. The Corporation Tax Return (Form CT600) is structured so that the tax liability can be worked out automatically. When HMRC sends you the notice to send it a Corporation Tax Return, there is a payslip attached to the bottom of the notice.

Payment must be made electronically, which means either using online banking, or making payment at a bank or Post Office.

What do I have to do about the Corporation Tax Return?

All Corporation Tax Returns must be submitted to HMRC electronically. Therefore, when the notice to complete a Corporation Tax Return arrives, we strongly suggest you send it to your accountant, if you have one.

What is the rate of Corporation Tax and how does the small company rate of tax work?

For accounting periods starting on or after 1 April 2015, the small company rate and the main rate of Corporation Tax have been unified at 20 per cent.

When is a company trading and how does this affect its tax position?

A company is trading once it has sold something. It's also trading if it has been incorporated and has begun to develop and manufacture goods or services. Any loss that it makes will be carried forward until it makes its first profit. The loss can then be used to reduce the first profits.

Do dormant companies have to pay Corporation Tax?

Dormant companies are, by definition, those that are doing nothing and, although a Corporation Tax Return may have to be submitted, there would be no profits and therefore no tax to pay.

Under recent legislation it's possible for a dormant company to do certain minor things (such as pay the annual return fee), but this doesn't include the earning of taxable profits.

What are 'associated' and 'subsidiary' companies?

Associated companies are those that are under common control or where one controls the other.

A subsidiary company is one that is either wholly or substantially owned by another company. A subsidiary company may surrender its losses to its holding company (or vice versa) thus allowing the holding company to set those losses off against its profits. This is called 'group relief'.

What is the significance of a 'close company'?

A close company is, broadly speaking, a company that is under the control of five or fewer 'participators'. A participator is a person having a share or interest in the capital or income of the company. It's defined broadly to include, for example, any loan creditor of the company and any person who possesses a right to receive or participate in distributions of the company. A quoted company is not a close company if more than 35 per cent of its voting shares are owned by the general public.

Close companies used to be subject to special provisions, but the only provision that applies now is where they make loans or distributions to their directors. When this happens tax has to be charged on the loan or distribution, unless the loan is repaid before the tax is due, i.e. nine months after the end of the company's financial year. If the loan is subsequently repaid, the company can get the tax back.

What is the difference between a public and a private company?

A public company is a company:

- the Memorandum of Association of which states it to be a public company;

- that has been registered as such;

- whose name ends 'public limited company' or plc;

- which has an allotted share capital of not less than £50,000 of which at least 25 per cent has been paid on issue.

All other companies are private companies. A private company that incorporates some but not all of these features remains a private company.

Note: Although private companies have advantages over public companies, trading under any sort of incorporated structure attracts extra hassle and administration. Professional advice must be sought.

What do UK companies with overseas income have to do about it?

A company that has overseas income has to pay Corporation Tax on the gross amount of such income, but double tax relief is usually available. If a UK company receives a dividend from an overseas company from which tax has been deducted, the gross dividend is included in the taxable profits. However, there are other rules and we do suggest that you refer to specialist advice for help.

What are the tax rules about companies buying their own shares?

In the case of a small company, it's frequently difficult for a buyer to be found for the shares of a shareholder who wishes to retire or sell up. There are now rules which enable companies to buy their own shares but, once again, we suggest that professional advice is sought on this. Briefly, the rules are that:

- the company must not be quoted and should be trading or be the holding company of a trading company;

- the purchase of the shares by the company must be mainly to benefit the trade of the company;

- the shareholder must be UK resident and must have owned the shares for at least five years. In addition, his shareholding must be substantially reduced and this usually means by at least 25 per cent;

- if the payment is used to pay Inheritance Tax within two years after death, the above provisions do not apply.

To the extent that the amount paid for the shares exceeds the amount originally subscribed, there is deemed to be a distribution or dividend payable by the company to the shareholder concerned. This would normally be taxed as income in his or her hands. However, if advance clearance is obtained from HMRC, it is possible to get this payment taxed as a capital gain which will usually be advantageous to the shareholder.

How do I pay myself from my company?

In principle, you can either pay yourself a salary (which could be in the form of a bonus or other remuneration) or, so long as you hold shares in the company and there are the profits out of which to pay it, you could be paid a dividend.

If you are paid a salary, normal PAYE rules apply. If you are paid a dividend, the company doesn't have to pay any tax over at the time of making the distribution. This is because dividends can only be paid out of profits which have already been taxed. In principle, dividends are a more tax-efficient way of withdrawing profits from a company than salary. If you have lent money to your company and that company wishes you to be able to withdraw some of that loan (to have it paid back), there would be no tax involved with any such repayment.

What are the tax rules about a company paying dividends?

The company accounts will show (hopefully) a profit. This profit figure will have deducted from it the amount of Corporation Tax that the company is due to pay on its profits. Whatever remains is added to the cumulative profits brought forward or deducted from the cumulative losses brought forward. A dividend can only be paid out of retained profits. If there are no retained profits – even though the company may have made a profit in its latest financial year – no dividend can be paid.

The company must be able to afford to pay a dividend to all of the holders of the class of shares on which the dividend is declared. This point is made as it is not possible for one shareholder to waive entitlement to a dividend and for another shareholder to therefore have a higher rate of dividend.

If there are undistributed profits brought forward, then these also can be distributed by way of a dividend.

If the company makes a loss, but there are greater undistributed profits brought forward than the loss, then a dividend can still be declared.

How does a company get relief for its losses?

This is a large subject, but we will try to give the basic rules as simply as we can.

A trading loss made in an accounting period can be set off against any other income and gains of the same period. Any remaining loss can then be carried back against the trading profits for the preceding year or it can be carried forward and set off against the trading profits of future years. A trading loss in the final period can be carried back for three years.

How does group relief for losses work?

The trading losses of members of a group of companies can be used to reduce the trading profits of other members of the group, provided that:

- a claim is made within two years of the end of the accounting period;

- the companies participating in the group relief claim are all based in the UK and the parent has at least 75 per cent interest in each of the subsidiaries, directly or indirectly. A company may be based outside of the UK without jeopardising the existence of a group but it may not itself participate in the relief.

Please note that even though the parent may only own 75 per cent of the shares, it's entitled to 100 per cent of the relief. Also note that capital losses cannot be group relieved.

There are complicated rules where a company joins or leaves a group during an accounting period – this is another reason for seeking professional advice.

How does a company pay Capital Gains Tax?

Companies pay Corporation Tax on their capital gains. Companies can still claim indexation relief (unlike individuals, partnerships and trusts).

Trading losses in accounting periods may be set off against not only gains, but also trading profits of the same period or indeed the previous period. Capital losses incurred by a company can only be offset against capital gains of the company in the same period or future accounting periods.

The Rollover Relief described on page 114 is also available to companies. In addition, if one company in a group has a gain, another company in the group can purchase a qualifying business asset and roll the gain into the purchase, deferring any charge to Corporation Tax.

Similarly, if one company has unused capital losses and another group company is to make a disposal which results in a capital gain, the company with the losses can be deemed to be making the disposal so that its losses can be used against the gain.

The rules are complicated and professional advice must be sought.

Can a director borrow money from his company?

In principle, it's unlawful for a director to borrow money from his own company. Small expense sums are allowed to be borrowed in advance. If the loan has not been repaid nine months after the end of the company's financial year, tax at the rate of 32.5 per cent has to be paid on the sum borrowed (this sum is repaid by HMRC when the loan is repaid and it would be reported on the next CT600 submitted after repayment). If no interest or a beneficial rate of interest is paid on the loan (unless the loan is for £10,000 or less), a benefit in kind arises on which the director must pay Income Tax and the company must pay Class 1A National Insurance contributions.

Do companies claim capital allowances in the same way as sole traders and partnerships?

The normal capital allowances and annual investment allowance rules for businesses apply to companies, but there are special rules and we suggest that professional advice is sought.

In a 'mixed partnership', where one of the partners is a company or a trust, you cannot use the annual investment allowance, only capital allowances.

Can loss-making companies claim cash back in lieu of their capital allowances?

If a limited company incurs expenditure on or after 1 April 2008 on energy-saving or environmentally friendly plant and machinery which is eligible for 100 per cent capital allowances, and makes a loss, then the loss arising from the expenditure can be surrendered for a cash payment from the government. The company will receive a 19 per cent tax credit on the loss surrendered up to a maximum of the higher of (a) the total of the company's PAYE and NIC liabilities for the period of the loss, or (b) £250,000.

For more information, you can visit the Enhanced Capital Allowances website at www.eca.gov.uk. This legislation has been extended and remains in place until 31 March 2018.

What are Personal Service Companies and how are they taxed (IR35)?

The so-called IR35 rules prevent someone (a worker) who works predominantly for just one business (a client) trading as a limited company (the intermediary) and then paying himself dividends from the profits, thus avoiding National Insurance altogether.

Before we outline the rules, here are some definitions:

A worker will be caught by the rules if he:

- trades as a limited company (the intermediary); and

- controls more than five per cent of the dividends; and

- receives or could receive payments from the intermediary which under normal circumstances would be paid to him as salary.

Partnerships are also caught if:

- the worker, together with his close family, is entitled to more than 60 per cent of the profits of the partnership; or

- most of the profits come from working for a single client; or

- a partner's profit share is based on his income from relevant contracts.

Now for the rules:

In the circumstances where a worker provides his services to one client for a contract lasting for more than a month, the rules state the following:

- You take the amount of cash and non-cash benefits received by the intermediary.

- You then deduct any salary (actual salary) paid by the intermediary to the worker.

- You also deduct an allowable expense claim, which is a flat rate allowance of a total of:

  - the business mileage allowances for travel to each engagement;

  - five per cent of the expenses paid by the intermediary for the contracts;

- • the expenses normally allowed to an employee;
- • the capital allowances normally allowed to an employee;
- • the employer's pension contributions;
- • the employer's National Insurance contributions.
- The balance (called 'deemed salary') is then treated as pay. Tax and National Insurance have to be applied accordingly.
- The tax and National Insurance arising on the balance are payable by 19 April after the year with interest running on late payments.
- Unpaid amounts can be recovered from the worker if the intermediary doesn't pay up.

There is one final twist: the deemed salary is not regarded as wages for the purpose of the National Minimum Wage, so the actual salary must be sufficient to meet the minimum wage requirements.

This is a nightmare, although it should be said that all other employees who are taxed under PAYE are following the proper rules, so why not these workers as well?

There are ways to escape from this net but space is not available here to explain what needs to be done. However, even if it's possible to escape, certain clients insist that their workers do trade as a limited company, to save themselves having to apply PAYE.

What is the special Corporation Tax treatment of research and development expenditure for small and medium-sized companies?

This is a very specialised area and there are a number of providers of advice and guidance in this field. The expertise mainly relates to what expenditure qualifies as research and development, and how direct and overhead costs, e.g. staff wages, are attributed to particular innovative projects.

If your company is spending money on R&D the tax breaks are really quite generous. From 1 April 2012, a company can claim 225 per cent of its qualifying revenue and expenditure against its profits. From 1 April 2015, this has been increased to 230 per cent. The government has also announced a publicity campaign aimed at small companies to increase awareness of the scheme.

It is also possible to 'exchange' the R&D relief for a tax credit, which can be set against the company PAYE liabilities.

CHAPTER 13

Non-residence, working overseas, etc.

What is the significance of my tax domicile?

Your domicile is the country which you regard as your natural home and the place where you intend to return in the event of going abroad. For most people it's the country of their birth and, unlike tax residence, it's not possible to have two domiciles under English law.

If non-domiciled individuals who have been resident for more than seven of the past nine years want to claim the remittance basis of assessment they will have to pay an annual charge of £30,000 on top of the UK tax on their overseas income and gains. From 6 April 2015, there is an increase in the annual charge to £60,000 for non-domiciled individuals who have been UK resident for 12 of the past 14 years. A new charge of £90,000 is being introduced for those who are UK resident for 17 of the previous 20 years. These charges will not apply if the unremitted income or gains are less than £2,000 and if this is the case, UK personal allowances and the annual capital gains allowance will also be available.

This is a complex area and anyone affected should seek specialist advice.

What is the Statutory Residence Test?

The Statutory Residence Test has been designed to provide greater certainty as to whether or not individuals are UK resident for tax purposes. This test does not have retrospective effect, but it could be the case that somebody who has previously been non-UK-resident becomes UK-resident following the introduction of this test.

There are a number of stages to the test and a variety of rules to apply to determine an individual's status. It is split into a number of components:

- Automatic Overseas Tests

- Automatic Residence Tests

- Sufficient Ties Test

The basic rules are that you are non-UK-resident in a tax year if you meet any of the Automatic Overseas Tests. But you are UK-resident if you do not meet any of the Automatic Overseas Tests and you meet one of the Automatic Residence Tests, or the Sufficient Ties Test.

Automatic Overseas Tests

If you meet any one of these tests, you are non-UK-resident:

1. You were resident in the UK for one or more of the previous three tax years and you spend fewer than 16 days in the UK in the tax year.

2. You were not resident in the UK for any of the three preceding tax years and you spend fewer than 46 days in the UK in the tax year.

3. You work full-time overseas throughout the tax year without any significant breaks, and:

   a. you spend fewer than 91 days in the UK in the tax year;

   b. the number of days in the tax year on which you work for more than three hours in the UK is less than 31.

If, having taken this test, you are not conclusively non-resident, then you must move on to the Automatic Residence Test.

Automatic Residence Tests

If you meet any one of these tests, you will be automatically UK-resident:

1. You spend 183 days or more in the UK in the tax year.

2. You have a home in the UK during all or part of the tax year. You will meet this test if there is at least one period of 91 consecutive days, at least 30 of which fall into the tax year, when you have a home in the UK in which you spend a sufficient amount of time and you either:

   a. have no overseas home; or

   b. have an overseas home or homes in each of which you spend no more than a permitted amount of time.

   If you have more than one home in the UK, you should consider each of those homes separately to see if you meet the test. You need only meet this test in relation to one of your UK homes.

3. You work full-time in the UK for any period of 365 days, with no significant break from UK work, and:

   a. all, or part, of that 365-day period falls within the tax year;

   b. more than 75 per cent of the total number of days in the 365-day period when you do more than three hours of work are days when you do more than three hours work in the UK;

   c. at least one day which is both in the 365-day period and in the tax year is a day on which you do more than three hours of work in the UK.

Sufficient Ties Test

If you do not meet any of the Automatic Overseas Tests or any of the Automatic Residence Tests, you should use the Sufficient Ties Test to determine your UK residence status for a tax year. You will need to consider your connections to the UK, called ties, and determine whether your ties, taken together with the number of days you spend in the UK, are sufficient for you to be considered UK-resident for tax purposes for a particular tax year.

If you were not UK-resident for any of the three tax years before the tax year under consideration, you will need to consider if you have any of these UK ties:

1. Family: spouse, civil partner, partner, or minor children, in the UK.

2. Accommodation: having accommodation in the UK which is available for a continuous period of at least 91 days and you spend at least one night there.

3. Substantive work in the UK: 40 working days or more (a working day is defined as more than three hours of work).

4. UK presence in the previous two tax years: more than 90 days in either of the previous two tax years.

5. More days spent in the UK in a tax year than in any other single country: this applies to leavers only and is designed to catch leavers who do not take up residence in any other country following a period of UK residence.

The number of days you spend in the UK in a tax year will dictate the number of UK ties that are needed for you to be UK resident.

Days in UK	Arrivers – not resident in the UK in previous three tax years	Leavers – resident in the UK in at least one of the previous three tax years
Less than 16	Always non resident	Always non resident
16 – 45 days	Always non resident	Resident only if at least four ties apply
46 – 90 days	Resident only if at least four ties apply	Resident only if at least three ties apply
91 – 120 days	Resident only if at least three ties apply	Resident only if at least two ties apply
121 – 182 days	Resident only if at least two ties apply	Resident only if at least one tie applies
183 days or more	Always resident	Always resident

What income is taxable and where?

If you are resident in this country, all normal taxable income, whether arising here or overseas, is taxable. However, if you are non-resident and you receive income from self-employment, partnerships or employment, all of which are carried out abroad, it will be tax free in this country. In fact, if you are non-resident, then the only income that is taxable in the UK is income arising in the UK, e.g. property income. The rules are complicated so any aspect that needs further consideration should be referred for professional advice.

What is 'double taxation relief'?

The UK government has entered into Double Tax Agreements with certain overseas countries (about 127 in all), the purpose of which is to prevent income and capital gains being taxed in both countries. So where income or capital gains have already been taxed in another country, in principle the foreign tax counts towards your UK tax bill. However, such overseas tax is not refundable if it exceeds the UK tax due.

When does someone who goes abroad become non-UK tax resident?

In principle, someone going to work full-time abroad under a contract of employment will be treated as non-resident from the date he leaves the UK. He must stay overseas for at least a full tax year. Visits to the UK are allowed but must be less than the permitted limit as specified in the calculation for split-year treatment. If you go abroad for any other reason, HMRC may give a temporary non-residence ruling and then review the position fully after three full years.

What tax do I pay on foreign income?

If you are a UK resident, you pay normal UK tax on income from abroad, but if any of that foreign income has already suffered Income Tax in the country of origin, then it's more than likely that double taxation relief will result in that tax going towards paying your UK tax bill. However, the foreign tax cannot be refunded if it exceeds your UK tax liability.

What tax do I pay on foreign pensions?

For people who are resident and domiciled in the UK, there is a ten per cent deduction permitted from their foreign pension before calculating the tax liability which arises from it. If the foreign pension is paid as a result of Nazi persecution, then no liability to UK tax arises.

What is the tax position on professions conducted partly abroad?

If you work in any profession that is conducted partly within this country and partly overseas, you will normally be assessed to UK tax on your entire profits and it's only if you conduct a separate profession entirely abroad that special rules will apply.

What tax do I pay on earnings from overseas employment?

Again this is a tricky area, if you go to work abroad part way through a tax year, you may qualify for split-year treatment. There are a number of circumstances where you might meet the criteria for split-year treatment, so we would advise you to seek professional help if you believe that this could apply to you.

What allowances can non-UK tax residents claim?

You may be able to claim UK tax allowances if you are not resident here. If you are eligible to claim, you will generally be given the same allowances (i.e. the personal allowance) as an individual resident here. The following can claim, as well as certain others:

• A resident of the Isle of Man or the Channel Isles

- A citizen of the Commonwealth
- A citizen of a state within the European Economic Area
- A present or former employee of the British Crown

If I go abroad, do I have to pay tax on the rent I receive from letting out my home while I am away?

You will be liable to UK tax on the net rental income (i.e. gross rents less allowable expenses). Strictly speaking, the letting agent, or the tenant if there is no letting agent, should deduct tax at basic rate before paying the rent to you. However, you can apply to HMRC for a certificate authorising rental payments to be paid without deduction of tax.

You will still be entitled to your personal allowance and it may be that some of the tax that is deducted can be refunded to you. We strongly suggest you employ the services of an accountant to look after this for you.

Can I go abroad to avoid Capital Gains Tax?

This is a complicated matter and professional advice should be sought. From 6 April 2015, if you are a non-UK resident you will be liable to Capital Gains Tax on gains made on the disposal of residential property which arise after that date. (See chapter 10, on Capital Gains Tax.) For any other gains, on shares for example, there is no CGT liability if you have been non-resident for at least five complete tax years.

What should I do if I have just arrived in the UK to take up work here?

In principle, you should contact the authorities or your employer will do this for you and from that day, even if it's the last day of the tax year, you will be entitled to the normal personal allowances. Equally, from that day you will be subject to Income Tax and National Insurance because you will be treated as a UK tax resident.

If you are self-employed or have income arising from a partnership or self-employment abroad or indeed interest arising abroad, then if you are UK resident but not UK domiciled, you will pay tax on income brought to the UK. If you are UK resident and UK domiciled, you will pay UK tax and may be able to claim double tax relief.

If I have just arrived in the UK, will the rest of my overseas income be taxed?

It depends on your residence and domicile status. See the final paragraph in the section above.

CHAPTER 14

Inheritance Tax

Note: All references to married couples include same-sex couples who have registered as civil partners.

What is Inheritance Tax?

Inheritance Tax is a tax on the transfer of wealth in certain defined circumstances. Succeeding Estate Duty and then Capital Transfer Tax, it was introduced in the 1986 Finance Act and, although it's a highly complicated tax, certain basic information is included in this book.

Inheritance Tax covers transfers of value on death and also chargeable lifetime transfers, such as transfers to discretionary trusts (unless they are set up for a disabled person). Chargeable transfers on death are taxed at nil on the first £325,000 and 40 per cent thereafter. Chargeable lifetime transfers are taxed at nil on the first £325,000 and 20 per cent thereafter. They may also be charged again on death if this occurs within seven years of the transfer, but credit will be given for any lifetime tax paid.

Transfers to individuals and non-discretionary trusts are called 'potentially exempt transfers'. No Inheritance Tax is payable on these, but if they occur within seven years of the transferor's death they are added to the value of his estate on death

It's worth bearing in mind that, starting at 40 per cent, Inheritance Tax is reaping far more for the Treasury than it used to and so it's a tax which should be attended to and, where possible, planning to minimise it should be put in place.

Deaths of armed forces personnel, emergency services personnel and humanitarian aid workers on or after 19 March 2014, caused or hastened by injury while on active service, are exempt from Inheritance Tax.

How and when is Inheritance Tax paid?

Inheritance Tax in respect of chargeable transfers on death is due six months from the end of the month of the death. If a chargeable lifetime transfer is made between 6 April and 30 September, the due date is 30 April in the following year. If the chargeable lifetime transfer is made between 1 October and 5 April, the due date is six months after the end of the month in which the transfer is made.

How should I approach the subject of Inheritance Tax?

As practising accountants, we hardly ever deal with Inheritance Tax matters ourselves, but we have been able to observe the way in which it's dealt with by other professional advisers.

Our view is that if you are worried about Inheritance Tax, you should not go to a solicitor for advice but rather to a specialist Inheritance Tax adviser. While we don't like commenting on other professionals, we think that the following analysis is fair and appropriate. Chartered Accountants in practice are extremely competent at Income Tax, Capital Gains Tax, Value Added Tax as well as other accounting functions, but on the whole we should not advise our clients on matters of law. When it comes to solicitors, while they are very competent at matters of law, in our opinion only those who have the appropriate training and experience should advise their clients on matters of tax and particularly Inheritance Tax, where we have seen a number of bad mistakes made by people who have not been properly trained, who 'didn't know what they were doing'. So our advice is that Inheritance Tax planning should be dealt with by a specialist in Inheritance Tax matters. This is how we run our practice and how we advise our clients whenever they need Inheritance Tax advice.

Should I make a Will?

We always ask our clients if they have made a Will and try to make sure that, if they haven't, they do so quickly. If you haven't made a Will, the chances are that, when you die, your assets won't go to the people you would like them to go to. It's not expensive drawing up a Will and we would strongly suggest you go to a solicitor to do so. However, in view of our comments about Inheritance Tax planning, we think it would be a good idea for you to ensure, before you visit the solicitor, that you have listed your assets, applied a rough valuation to them and seen if the Inheritance Tax bill for your estate is one that you are prepared to pay. If you are frightened by the size of the Inheritance Tax bill, then we suggest that you go to an Inheritance Tax specialist. Then, when you go to your solicitor, you can be armed with not only what you want to happen but also how you want the Inheritance Tax matters to be dealt with. If you don't do it this way round, you may find that you have a solicitor who thinks he knows about Inheritance Tax making all the plans for you and in our experience this can often end in problems. However, you do need to make a Will.

A template to help you work out your Inheritance Tax bill and plan to make a Will is provided at Appendix 7.

How do I choose my executors?

In our view, it's extremely important to appoint executors whom your survivors like. We have seen cases where the executors who have been appointed were not liked by the surviving spouse and the misery caused by the death of the testator was exacerbated by the insensitivity of the executors. Therefore, don't choose your own friends just because you like them. Make sure your spouse likes them too and is happy for them to be appointed.

The nil-rate band rules

The nil-rate band is £325,000. Married couples and civil partners inherit each other's unused element of the nil-rate band on first death. So, couples have a joint nil-rate band of £650,000. If the couple's joint estate falls within the joint nil-rate band, they no longer have to worry about Inheritance Tax.

For everyone else, including unmarried couples, siblings living together and carers who have lived in and inherited the family home, the nil-rate band is £325,000 each, but they have no joint band.

In the 2015 Summer Budget, the government announced it will phase in a new residence nil-rate band (RNRB) from 6 April 2017 when a residence is passed on death to a direct descendant. It will be £100,000 in 2017 to 2018; £125,000 in 2018 to 2019; £150,000 in 2019 to 2020; and £175,000 in 2020 to 2021. It will then rise in line with the Consumer Price Index (CPI) from 2021 to 2022. This will reduce the burden of Inheritance Tax for most families, by making it easier to pass on the family home to direct descendants without a tax charge.

How can I reduce Inheritance Tax?

This is such a big subject and the sums involved are so potentially enormous that we would not presume to give anything more than general advice in a book of this nature. However, there are certain general rules which we believe to be sound:

- Don't give everything away before you die; if you do and you keep on living, what will you live on?

- Consider taking advice from an Inheritance Tax specialist.

- Keep your Will up to date.

- Let your survivors know in advance if their lives are likely to be radically affected by your death. There is this problem that Wills generate great anticipation and anxiety and it's as well not to be too secretive about what you are proposing to do, so as to reduce extra stress and burdens on your survivors after you have died.

What are periodic charges?

Discretionary trusts are subject to a charge to Inheritance Tax every ten years. In many cases, the trust is able to take advantage of the nil-rate band

(£325,000 for 2016/17) and so no tax is payable. Any value in excess of this is charged at 30 per cent of the lifetime rate of 20 per cent, i.e. six per cent.

What is 'quick succession relief'?

If, after someone dies and Inheritance Tax is paid on his estate, a beneficiary dies within five years, quick succession relief applies and the tax payable on the second death is at a reduced rate.

How will assets be valued?

In principle, on death your assets are valued for Inheritance Tax purposes at what they might reasonably be expected to fetch on the open market. If, when an asset comes to be sold, the proceeds are less than the probate value, a claim can be made to reduce the IHT liability which arose on the higher value.

What are the first, essential IHT golden rules that I should follow?

1. **List your assets and decide to whom you would like them to pass.**

    Why not use the sheet in Appendix 7?

2. **Make a Will.**

    If you don't make a Will, the chances are that your assets on your death won't be distributed according to your wishes. However, before you make a Will, it would be a good idea to attend to item 1 so that when you visit your solicitor you can 'hit the ground running' and, at the outset, tell him what you want your Will to say.

3. **Calculate the Inheritance Tax due.**

    Again, use Appendix 7 for this purpose.

4. **Decide how seriously you view the impact of any Inheritance Tax payable.**

If you can tolerate the impact that Inheritance Tax may make on both your estate and your successors, then, so long as you have made a Will, you can probably rest at ease. However, having said 'probably', do remember that Inheritance Tax at 40 per cent can make a serious dent in your estate and, assuming you are not a tax expert, you might possibly overlook something and the situation may not be as favourable as you suppose. Accordingly, you may be well advised to take professional advice and get your Inheritance Tax calculation checked. As we say elsewhere in this chapter, the best professional advice on Inheritance Tax mitigation is to be gained from someone who specialises in Inheritance Tax mitigation and not necessarily from a high street accountant, financial adviser or solicitor. Therefore, choose your Inheritance Tax adviser very carefully.

5. **If you have an Inheritance Tax problem, then consult a suitably qualified adviser on how to mitigate the charge.**

Then, having received such expert advice, set about putting his recommendations in place.

6. **If you want to take some elementary steps to reduce the impact of Inheritance Tax, and if you do nothing else, please at least consider the following possible courses of action:**

   - If you are currently unmarried or not in a civil registered partnership and you are facing an Inheritance Tax bill on your death, then we strongly suggest you follow steps 1 to 4 above.

   - If you survive your spouse or civil partner, bear in mind that your executors will be able to utilise their unused nil-rate band.

   - Married couples and civil partners should review the ownership of the property they occupy.

   - When it comes to passing investments to your children, there are a number of excellent financial products (such as loan trusts and discounted gift schemes) which we have seen used to very good effect. One of the beauties of these schemes is that, while ensuring that the capital passes to the next generation in a tax efficient way, they can also (and usually do) increase your annual spending money.

   - If you can afford to do so, use the nil-rate band to good effect. If you were to give away 1/7 of the nil-rate band every year

(£46,428), by the time year seven had arrived, and assuming you are still alive, you would have given away at least £325,000 tax free. In year eight, the first gift would drop out of the equation, in year nine, the second, and so on. If both you and your spouse do this, then you can give away £92,856 per year. However, do take professional advice.

- If you invest in shares in unquoted trading companies (including shares listed on the Alternative Investment Market), once you have owned them for two years, they should qualify for 100 per cent Inheritance Tax Business Property Relief. However, be careful as the value of shares can just as easily go down as up.

- As part of your Inheritance Tax planning, try to ensure that you will have enough to live on!

What is a gift with reservation of benefit?

If you give an asset away but continue to enjoy a benefit from it, you are said to have reserved a benefit and have not effectively given the asset away. It will therefore still form part of your estate on death.

In the case of giving a house away but still living in it, this won't be a gift with reservation if you pay the full market rent on the house.

As we have explained elsewhere, there is an Income Tax charge on pre-owned assets. The giver has to pay tax on the annual value of the benefit he has retained.

CHAPTER 15

VAT

What is VAT?

Value Added Tax is a tax imposed when goods or services are sold. Any business which has a turnover in excess of £83,000 in the year beginning 1 April 2016 should – unless the business makes exclusively exempt supplies – register for VAT and add VAT to its VAT-able supplies. This threshold applies to a rolling 12 months' turnover, regardless of the accounting date of the business.

This is a complicated subject and anyone running a business with a turnover approaching £83,000 should seriously consider contacting an accountant to discuss whether he should register for Value Added Tax with HMRC.

In the case of businesses with a turnover in excess of £83,000, they certainly should take professional advice because they may be starting to get into deep trouble.

What are exempt supplies?

The following are exempt supplies:

- Land (this includes the sale of land and buildings, leases and rents)
- Insurance

- Postal services

- Betting, gaming and lotteries

- Finance

- Education

- Health and welfare

- Burial and cremation

- Subscriptions to trade unions, professional and other public interest bodies

- Sport, sports competitions and physical education

- Works of art – certain disposals exempted from capital taxes

- Fund-raising events by charities and other qualifying bodies

- Cultural services – admission to museums, exhibitions, zoos and performances of a cultural nature supplied by public bodies and eligible bodies

- Supplies of goods where input tax cannot be recovered

- Investment gold

- Cost sharing

What records do I need to keep if my business is VAT-registered?

We strongly suggest that you keep records, either on a computer or in a cash analysis book; all your VAT records should be kept for six years.

In addition to this, you need to keep your invoices on which you have claimed back VAT input tax. You also need to keep copies of your sales invoices on which you have recorded your output tax.

You have to remember that it's likely that you will be investigated by HMRC's officials more than once during the average life of a business. When they come to see you, they will be wanting to check that your accounts are in order and that your VAT Returns have been properly prepared. You should arrange your affairs in such a way that anyone can find his way from your original transactions through to the submissions to HMRC without too much difficulty. The technical term for this is an audit trail and we would strongly suggest that you ask a professional accountant for help in making sure that your records are complete and well filed.

How do I complete my VAT Return?

For most VAT-registered traders, HMRC needs just four figures for the VAT Return:

1. **Output VAT** (box 1). This is the total of the VAT you have charged on your sales invoices during the period. If you complete the VAT Return under the cash accounting rules (if your turnover is less than £1,350,000), then your output tax is calculated on the cash received during the period and not on the invoices issued. The figure must include any VAT scale charge for private motoring (see below).

2. **Input VAT** (box 4). This is the VAT that you yourself have been charged on your purchases, etc. during the period. If you are registered for VAT, then nearly all the VAT you have been charged can be included in this box. If you complete the VAT Return under the cash accounting rules, then your input tax is calculated on the cash paid during the period and not on the invoices received. You may not reclaim VAT on business entertaining, goods or services used privately or on the purchase of motor cars. If you lease a car which has any element of private use, you can only reclaim half the input VAT. If you reclaim VAT on fuel, you must add the scale charge for your vehicle to the output VAT in box 1 (see above). In addition, if you make some taxable and some exempt supplies, you may only be able to claim part of your input VAT.

3. **Total outputs** (box 6). This is the sum of the invoices you have issued to your customers (the sales of standard and zero-rated goods and services) during the period. (You should not include any exempt sales or any capital introduced.) This sum should exclude the VAT element. However, if you are cash accounting, you total the sum received from your customers during the period but exclude the VAT element.

4. **Total inputs** (box 7). This is the sum of the invoices you have received from your suppliers during the period. This sum should

exclude the VAT element. However, if you are cash accounting, you total the payments you have made for standard and zero-related purchases during the period, less the VAT element. You should not include any exempt purchases, nor any drawings.

You will notice that there are five other boxes on the VAT Return:

- Boxes 2, 8 and 9 affect few small traders; if they affect you, you should seek professional advice.

- The only other boxes that affect everyone are boxes 3 (the total of boxes 1 and 2) and 5 (the sum of box 3 less box 4 if there is net VAT to be paid to HMRC and the sum of box 4 less box 3 if there is net VAT to be reclaimed by you).

You must file the completed VAT Return electronically and make your VAT payment electronically by the seventh day of the month after the month following the end of your VAT period.

HMRC treat all cheques sent by post as having been received on the date when cleared funds reach the department's bank account.

Can you tell me about VAT online?

All VAT Returns should be completed and submitted online – but there are exemptions. You do not have to file online if either of the following applies:

- you're subject to an insolvency procedure; or
- HMRC is satisfied that your business is run by members of a religious society, whose belief prevents them from using computers.

Unfortunately, you must still file online even if you:

- don't own or have access to a computer that is connected to the internet;
- lack computer skills;
- disagree in principle with compulsory online filing.

If you feel you may require help, you should contact HMRC or a professional adviser.

What is the Fuel Scale Charge?

If you reclaim VAT on all your motor fuel including that used privately, you are deemed to be making a supply to yourself of the private fuel. This supply must have output tax on it, just like any other standard rated supply. HMRC has prescribed values for this supply, depending on the size of your car engine and the type of fuel used. The rates are shown in Appendix 11. It follows that, if the scale charge exceeds the value of the input tax you actually suffer on fuel purchases, you are better off not claiming input tax at all on your fuel.

What is Annual Accounting for VAT?

If your turnover is less than £1,350,000, you may apply to HMRC not to fill in quarterly VAT Returns but, instead, to:

- pay a sum to it by direct debit each month;

- fill in a VAT Return once a year; and

- settle up any over- or underpayment with it at the end of the year.

If you do this, you have two months in which to file your VAT Return and pay any VAT due rather than one. Once your turnover reaches £1,600,000, you are no longer eligible to be part of the scheme.

What is Cash Accounting for VAT?

If your turnover is less than £1,350,000, you may pay VAT only when your customers have paid you and not on the basis of the invoices you have raised, whether they have been paid or not. Equally, you may only claim input VAT once your purchase invoices have been paid.

Once your turnover reaches £1,600,000, you are no longer eligible to be part of the scheme.

What is the optional flat rate VAT scheme for small traders and is it worth joining?

This scheme is for businesses with an estimated VAT-taxable turnover – excluding VAT – in the next year of £150,000 or less. Once you join the scheme you can stay in it until your total business income is more than £230,000.

Those who join the scheme won't need to keep a record of VAT input tax. You simply charge VAT to your customers as at present and record the VAT inclusive total charged to customers. You don't need to keep any record of the input tax incurred on your purchases. You then look up on the list of flat rate percentages the rate applicable to your category of business and pay that percentage to HMRC.

Whether it would be worth your while joining the scheme will depend on your circumstances. To work out how you would be affected were you to join, you take your turnover for the last 12 months, add VAT and then apply the relevant percentage. If that is less than the total payments you have made to HMRC in the period, then you may be better off joining the scheme.

You will no longer be able to reclaim input VAT on your expenditure. There is an exception to this for capital expenditure in excess of £2,000, on which input VAT may be reclaimed in the normal way.

If you join the scheme within one year of registering for VAT, you can get a one per cent reduction in your flat rate for the first 12 months. There are planning opportunities available for traders who carry on more than one type of business and each would have a different flat rate percentage. The percentage to be used is that which would apply to the business whose activity accounts for the majority of the trade. Where the majority trade has a lower flat rate percentage than the secondary trade, there may be savings to be made.

If you want to join, you should telephone your local VAT office for an application form or download one from the HMRC website (VAT600 FRS – Application to join the Flat Rate Scheme).

Table of flat rate percentages by trade sector

Category of business	Appropriate percentage
Accountancy or book-keeping	14.5
Advertising	11
Agricultural services	11
Any other activity not listed elsewhere	12
Architect, civil and structural engineer or surveyor	14.5
Boarding or care of animals	12
Business services that are not listed elsewhere	12
Catering services including restaurants and takeaways	12.5
Computer and IT consultancy or data processing	14.5
Computer repair services	10.5
Dealing in waste or scrap	10.5
Entertainment or journalism	12.5
Estate agency or property management services	12
Farming or agriculture that is not listed elsewhere	6.5
Film, radio, television or video production	13
Financial services	13.5
Forestry or fishing	10.5
General building or construction services*	9.5
Hairdressing or other beauty treatment services	13
Hiring or renting goods	9.5
Hotel or accommodation	10.5
Investigation or security	12
Labour-only building or construction services*	14.5
Laundry or dry-cleaning services	12
Lawyer or legal services	14.5
Library, archive, museum or other cultural activity	9.5
Management consultancy	14
Manufacturing fabricated metal products	10.5
Manufacturing food	9

Manufacturing that is not listed elsewhere	9.5
Manufacturing yarn, textiles or clothing	9
Membership organisation	8
Mining or quarrying	10
Packaging	9
Photography	11
Post offices	5
Printing	8.5
Publishing	11
Pubs	6.5
Real estate activity not listed elsewhere	14
Repairing personal or household goods	10
Repairing vehicles	8.5
Retailing food, confectionary, tobacco, newspapers or children's clothing	4
Retailing pharmaceuticals, medical goods, cosmetics or toiletries	8
Retailing that is not listed elsewhere	7.5
Retailing vehicles or fuel	6.5
Secretarial services	13
Social work	11
Sport or recreation	8.5
Transport or storage, including couriers, freight, removals and taxis	10
Travel agency	10.5
Veterinary medicine	11
Wholesaling agricultural products	8
Wholesaling food	7.5
Wholesaling that is not listed elsewhere	8.5

When can I deregister?

If your turnover is not going to exceed £81,000 in the coming 12 months, you can apply for deregistration.

CHAPTER 16

Stamp Duty

What is Stamp Duty?

Stamp Duty is payable by the purchaser on transfers of shares and certain other documents and it's quite complicated trying to work out whether something attracts Stamp Duty or not.

When it comes to share transfers, the amount of Stamp Duty payable is 50p for every £100 and is rounded up to the nearest £5. Stamp Duty is not payable on the issue of shares.

Transfers that attract Stamp Duty of no more than £5 are exempt.

It might be helpful to include a list of the instruments which require stamping:

- Stock and share transfers
- Declarations of trust
- Certain proxy forms
- Tenancy agreements where the gross rent is more than £5,000 per annum and is for a six- or 12-month term

Certain Stock Transfer Forms only attract a fixed duty of £5, no matter what the transaction and these are listed on the Stock Transfer Form.

Transfers to, from or between trustees, transfers in connection with divorce, and transfers which are gifts don't attract Stamp Duty.

When and how is Stamp Duty paid?

Stamp Duty is assessed and paid by the person who is responsible for ensuring that it's paid. He sends the document to the Stamp Duty Office (your local Tax Office will tell you where this is) to be stamped and the document will be returned to you stamped with the amount that you have paid.

If you happen to be in London, it's well worth a visit to Bush House in The Strand to see the Stamp Duty Office because in there you will see stamping machines which were made 70 years ago, still going strong. Maybe one day stamping will become electronic in one form or another, but at the moment it's performed by what can only be described as 'Green Goddesses'.

What is Stamp Duty Land Tax?

Stamp Duty Land Tax (SDLT) is generally payable on the purchase or transfer of property or land in the UK, where the amount given is above a certain threshold. Most UK land and property transactions must be notified to HMRC on a Stamp Duty Land Tax Return within a certain time limit; even if no tax is due.

Various rules apply for working out how much, if any, SDLT is payable. The calculation – based on a value called the 'chargeable consideration' – can vary depending on whether the land is residential or non-residential, freehold or leasehold, or on other factors such as whether several transactions are linked.

There are also some types of transaction that are exempt from SDLT, or where reliefs can reduce the amount payable.

SDLT is charged as a percentage of the amount given for property or land when it is bought or transferred, unless there is a relief or exemption. Higher percentage SDLT rates apply to higher-value transactions.

The rates of SDLT are:

Property value	Charge for the 2016/17 tax year
£0 to £125,000	0%
£125,001 to £250,000	2%
£250,001 to £925,000	5%
£925,001 to £1.5m	10%
£1.5m plus	12%

From 4 December 2014, the rates of Stamp Duty only apply to the amount of the purchase price that falls within the duty band, making it more like the calculation of Income Tax.

From 1 April 2016, those buying an additional residential property will pay a higher rate of SDLT on the purchase, being 3 per cent higher than the usual levels. This is targeted at buy-to-let landlords, but catches ordinary individuals who are unable to sell their existing property before they buy a new property. If the original property is sold within 3 years from the date of purchase of the new property, the additional 3 per cent SDLT charge will be refunded. The purchase of property for less than £40,000 is not caught by this additional charge.

There is no change to the rates of SDLT on non-residential or mixed-use property. The rates applicable are:

Property value	Charge for the 2016/17 tax year
£0 to £150.000	0%
£150,001 to £250,000	1%
£250,001 to £500,000	3%
£500,001 plus	£4%

Since 19 July 2011, there has been a new SDLT relief when more than one dwelling is purchased. The rate of tax charged is determined by dividing the total consideration by the number of dwellings. However, there is a minimum rate of one per cent. Relief should be claimed on a Land Transaction Return.

From 1 April 2015, Land & Buildings Transaction Tax (LBTT) replaces SDLT in Scotland; further information is available on the Revenue Scotland website at www.revenue.scot/land-buildings-transaction-tax.

From 20 March 2014, if residential property is bought for more than £500,000 by a 'non-natural person' (i.e. a company, partnership including a company, or collective investment scheme) then SDLT is payable at 15 per cent. (See also page 98 for the Annual Tax on Enveloped Dwellings.)

CHAPTER 17

Tax Credits, Universal Credit and related matters

What are Child Tax Credit and Working Tax Credit?

Warning: The whole subject of tax credits is extremely complicated, both in terms of entitlements and withdrawal rates. We have done our best to reduce it to its simplest elements, but reading the following section needs a clear head! You also need to be aware that the whole system of tax credits is being phased out from October 2013 in favour of Universal Credits (see below). There have been delays encountered with the phasing-in of Universal Credits, but the process is still moving forwards across the country.

Working Tax Credit (WTC) is a means-tested non-taxable benefit for those in work on low incomes. The qualifying conditions are as follows:

- If you are single with one or more children, you need to work 16 or more hours per week; the same limit applies if you have a disability, or are aged over 60.

- If you are a couple with one or more children, you need to work 24 or more hours per week between the two of you.

- If you don't have children, you need to be over 25 years old and working more than 30 hours per week.

Child Tax Credit (CTC) is paid to the main carer of the child or children. It can be claimed by families with at least one child. The income threshold above which tax credits start to be clawed back is £16,105 and the withdrawal rate is 41 per cent, i.e. for every pound over the threshold you earn, you will lose 41p in tax credit. However, your income can be higher than this if you pay for childcare, have a disabled child, have more than one child, or you yourself are disabled. It provides support for:

- Children until 1st September after their 16th birthday.

- Children aged 16 to 19 who are in full-time 'non advanced' education, i.e. studying at least 12 hours per week towards a qualification at A level, NVQ3 or below, or those receiving approved training under unwaged work-based training programmes.

- Children aged 16 to 19 who have left full-time education but don't have a job or training place and have registered with the Careers Service or Connexions Service and are not claiming Income Support or Tax Credits in their own right.

What if my circumstances change?

You must tell the Tax Credit Office if you:

- marry or live with someone as a couple;

- separate;

- have a new baby;

- stop paying for childcare for at least 4 weeks, or childcare costs reduce by £10 per week for at least 4 weeks in a row.

The following changes regarding your child (or children) need to be notified to the Tax Credit Office within 1 month, if they:

- leave home;

- die;

- leave education or training which counts for CTC purposes;

- begin training that is provided as part of their job;

- get a paid job and they are usually paid to work more than 24 hours in a week;

- start to claim benefits or tax credits in their own right.

And if within three months they:

- stay on in education or training that counts for tax credit purposes after they reach 16;

- stop education or training that counts for tax credit purposes, but register with the Careers Service or Connexions.

If you have not made a claim for tax credits before because you thought that perhaps you did not qualify, it may be worth making a protective claim. Normally, any claim you make can only be backdated for 3 months. If however you make a protective claim at the beginning of the tax year, even though you may get no benefit in the short term, if your circumstances change for the worse, due to redundancy for instance, you would be entitled to claim for the full year.

What next?

HMRC are renewing awards for the year ending 5 April 2017 and finalising new awards for the year ending 5 April 2016.

Credits for the year ending 5 April 2017 will be based on income for the year ending 5 April 2016. The following should be noted:

- If requested, details of income and circumstances should be submitted by 31 July 2016.

- The details you provide should relate to the period of the claim, which may not necessarily coincide with the tax year; for instance, if you had a baby during the year.

If you only receive the family element of CTC, you won't be asked to provide details of income and your claim will carry on as before. However, if your circumstances have changed, you must notify the Tax Credit Office. Remember, any increases in credits are only backdated for three months.

You can request a claim form by telephoning 0845 300 3900 or you can apply online at www.hmrc.gov.uk.

What is Universal Credit?

The purpose of Universal Credit is to simplify the benefit system and make it easier for people to take jobs, even for brief periods, without running the risk of losing out financially.

Universal Credit replaces: Child Tax Credit, Housing Benefit, Working Tax Credit, Income Support, income related Employment Support Allowance (ESA) and income based Jobseeker's Allowance.

Universal Credit does not replace: Attendance Allowance, Bereavement benefits, Child Benefits, Carer's Allowance, Council Tax Benefit, Maternity Allowance, Statutory Maternity Pay, Statutory Sick Pay, Disability Living Allowance, Contributory Employment Support Allowance, Contributory Jobseekers Allowance, Pension Credit, Industrial Injuries Disablement benefit, Personal Independence Payment & War Pensions.

Universal Credit is payable on a monthly basis to a household regardless of whether the household comprises one individual, a couple or a family. There is a main element plus additional elements which have to be applied for if a household qualifies. These elements are: child and disabled child element, childcare element, carer element, limited capability for work element and housing element.

Universal Credit has a cap applied to make it impossible for people to get more by claiming benefits than the average net weekly wage. For a household this figure is £500 per week and for single adults the cap is £350 per week. The childcare element of the Universal Credit will be excluded from the benefit cap.

Some households are exempt from the benefit cap, namely, those households where Disability Living Allowance or Attendance Allowance are claimed.

One of the major changes is that, with a few exceptions, all claimants are required to enter into a binding commitment that, in exchange for receiving Universal Credit, they undertake to look for and take on any work that is available.

There is a lot of 'small print' relating to what jobs have to be accepted and there are also sanctions for those who do not comply with their commitment in this regard.

Concerns have been expressed by certain groups about this new legislation, but equally, the huge cost of paying benefits has to be reined in; so that only the most needy and deserving are protected, and those who can work should be encouraged and supported to do so.

What are Pension Credits?

Pension Credit is an income-related benefit made up of two parts: Guarantee Credit and Savings Credit.

Guarantee Credit tops up your weekly income if it is below £155.60 (single person) or £237.55 (couple).

Savings Credit is an extra payment for people who have saved some money towards their retirement. This can be up to £13.07 (single person) or £14.75 (couple).

The age at which you can claim these credits is rising in line with the women's state pension age. You can claim on the Pension Credit claim line: 0800 99 1234.

What counts as income for Pension Credits?

State pension; occupational pension and private pensions; most Social Security benefits; net earnings from employment or self-employment less an allowance for half of any pension contributions made; and Working Tax Credits.

There is an 'assumed income' of £1 for every £500 (or part thereof) of capital you have over £10,000.

Contact the Pension Credit claim line for more details on 0800 99 1234.

What is adjusted net income?

In certain circumstances, your entitlement to certain allowances or benefits is affected by the amount of your income and certain payments that you make. If you are in any of the following categories, you need to calculate your adjusted net income:

- You are over 65 and your income exceeds £27,700 (2016/17).

- Regardless of your age, you have income in excess of £100,000.

- You have income over £50,000 and you or your partner claims Child Benefit.

1. Add together your total gross taxable income from:

    - Earnings (including employment benefits)

    - Profits from self-employment

    - Taxable social security benefits

    - Pensions

    - Savings income (interest, dividends and property rental income)

2. Deduct any trading or property losses which are relievable.

3. Deduct any gross paid pension contributions (usually old Retirement Annuity policies).

4. Deduct grossed-up Gift Aid donations, i.e. the amount you paid plus basic rate tax relief – £1 grosses up to £1.25.

5. Deduct grossed-up pension contributions which have been paid net of basic rate tax relief.

6. Deduct payments of up to £100 paid to trade union or police organisations for superannuation, life insurance or funeral benefits.

The net result of these adjustments is your adjusted net income.

What is the high income Child Benefit charge?

Historically Child Benefit has been paid to all families with children regardless of how much income the household has. From 7 January 2013, while Child Benefit will continue to be paid, it is progressively clawed back if either partner has income in excess of £50,000 per year. The claw-back recovers 1 per cent of the child benefit paid for every £100 that income exceeds £50,000. Therefore, all of the Child Benefit is effectively lost when income exceeds £60,000.

It may be regarded as unjust that one household with two working partners each earning exactly £50,000 will still be entitled to the full amount of Child Benefit, but a household where only one partner works and earns £60,000 will not be due any.

If your income is between £50,000 and £60,000, you should continue to claim Child Benefit and accept that some of this will effectively have to be paid back to HMRC. However, if you are not already within the Self-Assessment regime (i.e. you do not complete a Tax Return every year) then you should contact HMRC and ensure that they issue a Tax Return to you.

If you earn over £60,000, you should elect to stop receiving Child Benefit. However, even if you stop claiming benefit, if you find out at the end of the tax year that in fact your income is less than £60,000 you will still qualify for some Child Benefit.

To determine whether your income exceeds £50,000 per annum, please refer to the section 'What is adjusted net income?' opposite, which outlines the issues which can affect your income calculation.

CHAPTER 18

Other tax issues

Tax-planning dos

- Consider buying your own house as soon as you can. Any capital gain on your private residence will be tax free. However, by the same token there are no tax allowances for any losses on sale.

- Make sure you have got good pension and life assurance cover and keep the situation constantly under review.

- Make use (if you can afford to) of the £3,000 tax-free annual capital transfer (i.e. give this sum away Inheritance Tax-free each year) and, if you did not use up last year's allowance, you can give away an additional £3,000.

- Always claim your personal and other tax allowances. This should normally be dealt with for you by HM Revenue & Customs (HMRC) but you should keep the matter under annual review (e.g. have you passed retirement age?).

- Claim all business expenses you are entitled to against any business income – always keep a chit for petty cash expenses. If you don't, how will your accountant know you have incurred that particular expense?

- Pay your spouse properly for any work done in your business. In the 2016/17 tax year, remember, they can earn £11,000 tax free, although payments over £155 per week (£8,060) will involve employer's

National Insurance contributions being due. The employee will also pay National Insurance if their earnings are over £156 per week.

- Consult with your stockbroker in order to make sure you take advantage of the annual £11,100 Capital Gains Tax exempt amount, i.e. if you can make a gain of this size it will be tax free.

- Make a Will. You can create one inexpensively using Lawpack's *Last Will & Testament Kit* or you can take legal advice.

- Think carefully about providing funds to pay any Inheritance Tax on death (term assurance isn't very expensive).

- Plan ahead and, wherever possible, let your accountant know of your plans/wishes so that you can be advised on any tax implications.

- Divide your assets and the related income with your spouse so that the best use is made of Income Tax lower and basic rate bands. If one spouse/civil partner is not utilising all of their personal allowance, look at transferring the permitted amount to the other spouse/civil partner. Note that the recipient must only be liable to basic rate tax.

- Let an independent financial adviser give you the equivalent of a financial 'medical examination'.

- Ask your accountant to give you a rough idea of your tax liability in January and July each year. Then divide the sum by 12 and start saving up for it by transferring the monthly figure to a deposit account. This way paying tax is much less painful.

Tax-planning don'ts

There is a lot of what one might call 'pub chat' about tax – particularly on the subject of avoiding tax – and quite often the apparent expert is not giving the full picture. This is our attempt to give the tax novice some basic tax information so that he can tell whether the information coming across the crowded smoke-free room (or wherever) is accurate.

1. Don't avoid receiving income because it will have to have tax paid on it. If you earn £1 and pay the taxman 20p, you are still left with 80p and that is 80p more than you started out with. Whether you are

prepared to do the work for a net benefit of 80p or whatever is another matter. The main argument, often put forward, that you won't be able to afford to pay the tax on any extra income is a false one. If you receive income and pay tax on it, you are left with something. If you don't receive the income in the first place, you will be left with nothing.

2. Don't put tax saving first. Always put sound commercial or family considerations first and then fit the tax implications into what you want to do. If you own a business which is making money and paying tax, the key fact is that your business is making money. If your business is losing money and paying no tax, then the thing to concentrate on is not how marvellous it is that you are not paying tax but how vital it is to turn the business around and start making money. In the same way, but on a personal level, don't emigrate to a tax haven in order to save tax. Emigrate to a tax haven if you wish but your reason for doing so must not be to save tax but instead because you would rather live there than in the UK. If you don't like the place, why go to live there? Thus plan to do what you want to do first and then fit the tax implications into the picture.

3. Don't enter into tax-saving schemes, on the advice of either an accountant or anyone else, that run a long time. The law can change, your circumstances can change and either could make a nonsense of a long-term plan.

4. Don't automatically trust trusts. Be very careful about putting your money into trusts (see chapter 11).

5. Don't give all your money away in order to save Inheritance Tax. If you do, what will you live on?

6. Don't make your affairs too complicated. Keep your affairs simple and flexible so that you can (a) understand what is going on and (b) make any changes as and when you want.

7. Don't try to cheat the taxman. Be honest in all your dealings. Keep proper records of all your transactions, especially cash receipts, and declare everything properly. If you don't, you will be found out.

Tax-saving tips

For employers, employees and company directors

- Shares: companies can offer shares to staff through a share option or share incentive scheme. The rules are complicated, but the chances of acquiring wealth in a tax-efficient way are very real. Talk to an accountant first.

- Company car: this has become less popular as the taxable benefit of having a car has increased so much in recent years that it's often better to give back the car and have extra salary instead. However, if you are prepared to drive a smaller highly fuel-efficient car, it may still be beneficial to have a company car.

- Company fuel: this is now so heavily taxed that it will rarely be beneficial for a company to provide fuel to its employees. You should ensure that there is an agreement in writing which requires you to reimburse your company for any private fuel used. Better still, buy your own fuel and reclaim from the company that which is used for business.

- Cheap loans to employees: no taxable benefit arises in the case of a loan of up to £10,000.

- In general, all benefits are taxable, but meals provided free of charge (or at low cost) in a canteen on the firm's premises are not taxable if they are available to staff generally.

- HMRC's practice is not to tax expenditure of up to £150 per head on the annual Christmas party or a similar function (as long as it's open to all staff).

- Accommodation: a company may purchase a house for an employee to live in rent free. There may be a small amount of tax due on the value of the accommodation, etc., but the charge will be small in proportion to the benefits provided.

- Tax is not payable on financial rewards to staff for suggestions they may make on the running of a business. However, such 'suggestions schemes' must meet certain requirements.

- Incentive awards: employees can be given non-cash awards for meeting certain targets and, in addition, any tax that these might attract can be paid by the employer on the employees' behalf.

- Pension schemes: employers can consider making pension schemes non-contributory. This way they can reduce payments they make to staff by the amount of the pension contributions the staff members have been making (in other words, the member of staff would be no worse off as a result of this), but the company would have less National Insurance contributions to pay on the lower salary figure.

- Company directors will be able to save themselves a little tax in the form of National Insurance contributions for themselves, if instead of receiving their pay in the form of salary they were to receive the equivalent sum in the form of rent for the company's use of property owned by the director, dividends on shares or interest from the loan made by the director to the company. However, you should seek professional advice.

- Loans to directors: it's illegal under company law for a company to lend any director money and, even if it's done, there are heavy tax penalties attached to this. Do consider the following points:

  1. You can arrange the capital structure of the company so that at least part of your investment is by way of a loan account against which you may be free to draw.

  2. It may be possible to keep certain assets (e.g. property used by the business) outside the company.

- Other benefits: provide tax-free benefits to your employees such as childcare, sports or recreation facilities.

For those moving house while changing jobs

If you move home in order to take up new employment, or even a new post within your existing organisation, the following costs can be reimbursed by your employer without any Income Tax charge arising, up to an overall maximum of £8,000:

1. Bridging finance

2. Legal and professional fees and Stamp Duty

3. Travel and hotel costs

4. A reasonable subsistence allowance

5. A disturbance allowance (e.g. removal costs and insurance)

For those about to retire or who are retired

Golden handshakes – advance tax planning

*   You might ask your employer to pay part of any payment over £30,000 into your pension (within the limits of the scheme). HMRC accepts that no tax charge arises on such payments and this could enhance the tax-free lump sum you receive from the scheme.

*   If you are retiring and your total income will be significantly lower after retirement, it may be better to retire shortly after 5 April so that the taxable part of your golden handshake may be charged at a lower tax rate.

For the over 65s

Successive increases in the personal allowance, culminating in the 2016/17 figure being £11,000, mean that the old 'age allowances' are no longer applicable.

For the self-employed

The self-employed have considerably more flexibility in their tax-saving arrangements than employees, and those who are self-employed are probably well aware of the sort of advantages they may legitimately take. However, here are a few that should not be overlooked:

- If you are starting in business and need to draw all your profit to fund your living expenses, it may not be advisable to form a limited company straight away. As a self-employed trader, you have more flexibility and lower administrative costs. You can always incorporate later.

- A pension scheme is a most efficient way of diverting surplus profits into a tax-free lump sum and pension for the future.

A list of the types of expenses generally allowed is on pages 71 to 76.

For personal taxpayers – particularly higher-rate taxpayers

For those with high income (i.e. into the 40 and 45 per cent tax bands), and particularly if it's surplus to requirements, funds can be diverted to the following havens for tax advantages either on initial payment or at a later date:

- Life assurance – investing in a 'with profits' endowment policy that will run for at least ten years can produce a good tax-free return.

- National Savings Certificates – these can produce a good tax-free income. It's always a good idea to keep aware of what National Savings and Investments have on offer.

- Perks in quoted shares – many quoted shares now offer perks to their shareholders and these are entirely tax free.

- National Insurance – if you have more than one source of employment earnings and you are in danger of paying more than the maximum, why not defer Class 1 contributions on one of the employments to avoid making an overpayment?

- Pension contributions.

- The Enterprise Investment Scheme – you can invest up to £1,000,000 in Enterprise Investment Scheme (EIS) shares and you will get Income Tax relief of 30 per cent on that amount. If you hold the shares for three years, you get full Capital Gains Tax relief on sale.

  There is a 'carry back' facility that allows all of the cost of shares acquired in one tax year to be treated as though the shares had been acquired in the preceding tax year.

You must hold your Enterprise Investment Scheme shares for at least three years or the relief will be withdrawn.

Any loss you make on the sale of the shares is available against either capital gains or income.

You must not be connected with the company (i.e. hold over 30 per cent of the shares or be an employee) although you can become a director of the company and still qualify for EIS relief as long as you were not connected with the company before the shares were issued.

Deferral relief: in addition to the above, if you have made a capital gain this year, and if you reinvest all that gain in the purchase of EIS shares, you can thereby defer all the Capital Gains Tax payable this year on that gain until you sell your EIS shares.

- Seed Enterprise Investment Scheme (SEIS) – you can invest up to £100,000 in the year and get 50 per cent Income Tax relief on the investment. You can backdate the claim to the previous tax year. Providing you have claimed and been granted Income Tax relief on the investment, you can claim 50 per cent reinvestment relief on capital gains. Providing the investment is held for at least three years and the rules of the investment adhered to, there is no Capital Gains Tax on the proceeds.

- A Venture Capital Trust (see page 102).

For low earners

Young earners

Young people starting in employment have little scope for tax saving (usually because they have a low income), but they should not overlook the favourable Capital Gains Tax treatment available for those who purchase their main residence. Very few people have ever regretted purchasing their own residence.

Other low earners

Don't forget, if you are a low earner, whether in employment or self-employment, you may be able to avoid either Class 1 or Class 2 National Insurance contributions. You should not claim exemption from Class 2 contributions on the basis of low earnings unless you are already paying contributions on another source of income. If you don't pay, you build up no entitlement to benefits or pension rights; £2.80 per week is a small sum to pay to safeguard this entitlement (see page 31).

Tax-savings tips for children

Surplus after-tax income transferred by parents to their children is usually non-taxable in the hands of the child. However, where children earn income exceeding £100 in any tax year on capital provided by their parents, the whole income will be counted as that of their parents.

From 6 April 2016, all children's bank and building society accounts will be paying gross interest. You should compare the rates offered with Junior ISAs.

The Child Trust Fund (CTF) was a tax-free savings scheme designed for children. The government contributed £250 for children born between 1 September 2002 and 2 January 2011 and a further £250 (£500 for lower-income families) at the age of seven. The child was entitled to the fund at the age of 18 and there was no restriction on how he used the money. Children with a pre-existing CTF can continue to receive up to £1,200 per annum into their fund. CTFs were replaced by Junior ISAs on 1 November 2011 and provide all parents with a clear and simple way to save for their children's future. Children under the age of 18 who do not have a Child Trust Fund (CTF) are eligible for Junior ISAs. Parents can save up to £4,000 a year tax-free into these accounts. Funds in a Junior ISA are locked in until age 18 and roll over into an adult ISA on maturity, to help foster a long-term savings habit among young people.

Capital Gains Tax planning

Note: Spouses include same-sex registered civil partners.

* For married couples each spouse will be taxed on his or her own gains and will receive a non-transferable annual amount of £11,100.

* Do remember to maximise the benefit of your annual exempt amounts. To this end you could delay disposals until after the next 5 April if you have already used your current exemption or, alternatively, bring forward planned disposals to before 6 April if you have not yet used your exemption, or split the disposals of some asset, such as blocks of shares, to straddle 5 April in order to obtain the benefit of two years' exemptions.

* Consider whether you can wait until after 5 April to make the sales so as to delay the tax payment by a further 12 months.

* Assets of negligible value: if you hold an asset (e.g. shares in a company) which has lost most of its value, you may be able to claim the capital loss now against any capital gains. Ask HMRC if they will allow the loss.

* Loans and guarantees: you may obtain relief for losses on loans and guarantees made to people who have used the money wholly for the purpose of their business. Relief is not available if the loss or guarantee arises through your own act or omission or where the borrower is your husband or wife.

* No capital gain or loss arises on gifts between husband and wife, but the recipient takes over the other spouse's acquisition date and original value.

* Gifts to charities: because these are exempt from Capital Gains Tax it's often better, if you intend making a charitable donation of an asset which would realise a gain on disposal (e.g. shares), to consider donating the asset rather than the equivalent amount of cash. The charity may subsequently sell the shares and realise the gain free of tax because of its privileged status.

* Holdover relief for gifts: this is restricted to business assets, heritage property and property on which there is an immediate charge to Inheritance Tax.

* Don't always claim holdover relief – it's sometimes cheaper to pay a small amount of Capital Gains Tax than to hold over the tax bill of

some considerably greater sum to the future.

- All gifts are exempt from Stamp Duty.

- If you have assets which you expect will increase in value over a period of time, consider giving them to your children now.

- Main residence: no Capital Gains Tax is payable on the disposal of your home. Taking in a lodger doesn't affect your main residence relief but letting the property can. There are additional reliefs available for those who let out a property which has at some time been the only or main residence.

Inheritance Tax planning

- Married couples and civil partners should remember the doubling up of the nil-rate band. Each couple has a joint tax-free band of £650,000.

- It's possible to give away £325,000 every seven years without a charge to Inheritance Tax arising. However, there may be Capital Gains Tax on a non-cash gift, so take professional advice.

- There is tapering relief on the Inheritance Tax attributable to gifts so that, as the years up to seven slip by, the tax bill can reduce significantly.

- It's important to remember, in planning to reduce the Inheritance Tax bill upon your death, not to give away too much unless you can genuinely afford to do so. If you wish to make a gift of your family home but also wish to continue living in it, you must either pay full market rent for the privilege or consult a specialist Inheritance Tax adviser, who may be able to provide a sophisticated planning scheme to circumvent the 'reservation of benefit' rules. With no Capital Gains Tax arising on death it's sometimes better to let properties pass on death rather than before. However, this matter must be carefully weighed up before a decision is made.

- Lifetime gifts: gifts between husband and wife are exempt from Inheritance Tax.

- Remember, you can give away the annual Inheritance Tax-exempt sum of £3,000, which may be doubled up if exemption was not used in the previous year.

- Gifts of up to £250 per year to an individual are tax free.

- Gifts out of surplus income are tax free; take professional advice on this.

- Wedding gifts up to certain limits are tax free.

- Term assurance written in trust is a sensible means of protecting a gift that has been made should tax become due as a result of death within seven years.

- Make a Will and build the necessary tax-planning points into it. Discuss this with your solicitor, but see an Inheritance Tax specialist first.

- Special reliefs: generally, business assets attract some measure of relief, as does woodland and agricultural property. Agricultural property without a right to vacant possession may attract a lower rate of relief.

- Doubling up the main residence relief: it doesn't make good sense for you to buy a house or flat for your adult children to live in since any gain you make on its subsequent sale will be chargeable to Capital Gains Tax. Instead, consider providing your child with the necessary funds to make the purchase in his own name and you could do this by making an interest-free loan which you reduce each year by the annual £3,000 exemption.

- Incorporation of a growing business: it may be advantageous to give shares in the company to your children and/or grandchildren soon after incorporation when their value is relatively low.

Notable tax dates

See Appendix 9.

What is the difference between tax 'avoidance' and tax 'evasion'?

The short answer is that tax evasion is unlawful and tax avoidance is permissible. An example of tax evasion is deciding not to give HMRC details of all your sales (to pocket the cash and not tell anybody about the sales). This is fraudulent and will be heavily punished by the authorities when they discover it. Tax avoidance is taking the necessary legal measures to reduce your tax liabilities to the lowest permissible figure. For example, you may decide to invest in tax-free investments, such as ISAs, rather than in an investment which produces income that is taxable. However, remember that HMRC has certain anti-avoidance provisions to prevent tax being saved as a result of certain activities (e.g. inventing artificial transactions in land). Unfortunately, politicians and others who should know better sometimes confuse the two terms. Of late, there has been much discussion in the media about tax avoidance, and although legal, this too is becoming socially unacceptable. In our view, if tax law were simplified and clarified there would be far fewer loopholes to be exploited.

How should I deal with the Tax Office?

When we began in practice, some 40 years ago, HMRC's staff were portrayed as ogres and inspectors were regarded as 'the enemy'. In fact, in our long years of practice, we have always found we have enjoyed good relations with the Inspectors of Taxes and these bad reputations were both unkind and totally misleading.

While almost all HMRC staff try to be helpful and courteous in their dealings with the public, there is no doubting that dealing with HMRC is becoming much more difficult. It can take a very long time to get through by phone, most if not all of the public enquiry centres have been closed, and their website, while good in parts, can be cumbersome to deal with. There seems to have been a clear policy decision to try to cut costs by reducing the amount of direct dealings HMRC has with the public. Maybe we should all go back to writing letters to HMRC as this is less vexatious to the spirit than their awful automated telephone answering system which never seems to deal with the particular query one has.

Should I use an accountant?

The arrival of self-assessment was, we suspect, originally intended to do away with the accountancy profession. After all, self-assessment implies that the tax laws are so simple that you can 'do it yourself'.

The reality, and we feel that the answers given in this book prove that what we are about to say is correct, is that self-assessment has added to the complications and responsibilities and our view is that anyone having to fill out a Tax Return should seriously consider using the services of an accountant. Not only is life more complicated, but there are now penalties which were not in place before the arrival of self-assessment.

One of the big headlines following the Budget of 2015 was that Tax Returns would become a thing of the past. If you listened to the hype, you might have thought that you would never have to complete a Tax Return again. Unfortunately, the headlines and hype do not really convey the full truth. While the paper Tax Return, or its electronic equivalent, might be being phased out, people will instead have an electronic 'digital tax account'. The plan is for information already held by HMRC to be shown automatically, so that the taxpayer only has to fill in any missing information. While anything that makes a taxpayer's life simpler is to be applauded, responsibility for checking that HMRC's details are correct will still lie with the taxpayer. Fortunately, it will be possible to give your authorised agent access to your digital account.

When using an accountant you should always:

- ensure that the first meeting is free, so that you don't have to part with any money until you know whether you like the person or not;

- ask him to quote for fees upfront and ask him if it's an all-inclusive service.

For far too long professional accountants and solicitors have churned out bills to their clients based on the hours worked multiplied by the hourly rate. We believe that this approach is totally unfair to the client because the accountant never knows how big the bill is going to be. Instead, we believe that quotations should be made upfront and they should be stuck to, and that the professional should take more risk than has been the case.

How should I handle tax investigations?

HMRC is very successful at collecting additional tax through its tax investigations and we can all expect an HMRC inquiry into our affairs.

Self-assessment has given tax officers the power to make random tax inquiries. In effect, this means that they have more scope than ever to initiate tax investigations as you may now be investigated even if you have kept proper records.

While no taxpayer will be exempt from a random audit (whether he is an individual or a business), if his accounting and tax records are in good order and if the self-assessed tax liabilities have been calculated accurately and paid on time, he should have little to fear.

When you receive notice that an inquiry has begun, you should respond promptly, courteously and co-operatively. We would normally suggest you seek the services of a qualified accountant.

How do I appeal against a tax demand if I think it's too high?

If you think HMRC has made a mistake in your tax calculation, then you should contact HMRC within 30 days of the date of issue of the calculation and ask for an explanation of the figures. If this does not settle matters, you should put your reasons for believing that the calculation is wrong in writing and ask for the matter to be reviewed again at a more senior level. It may also be worth checking your records to ensure that you are actually correct and have not made an error. We are all human and can all make mistakes.

If you are not satisfied with their explanation, or you think that there must be an underlying problem which needs special attention, then you should consult a professional accountant and he will do the necessary.

What support is there for businesses struggling to pay their tax on time because of the recession?

On 24 November 2008, HMRC introduced a dedicated Business Payment Support Service designed to meet the needs of all businesses and individuals affected by the recession. Unfortunately, it is taking far longer than anticipated for the economy to flourish and so there is still an important role to be played by this part of HMRC.

If you're worried about not being able to meet Income Tax, National Insurance, VAT or other payments owed to HMRC, or you anticipate that you can't afford to make payments that are becoming due, you can call its Business Payment Support Service seven days a week. The staff will review your circumstances and discuss temporary options tailored to your business needs, such as arranging for you to make payments over a longer period. They will not charge additional late payment surcharges on payments included in the arrangement, although interest will continue to be payable on those taxes where it applies. The number to call is 0300 200 3835.

What electronic services does HMRC offer?

Whether you are a private individual who has to submit a Tax Return or in business whether incorporated or not, it is becoming increasingly likely that you will be dealing with HMRC electronically. Indeed, for businesses, any element of choice may already have been taken out of your hands.

Some of the more popular online services are as follows:

- Submitting Self-Assessment Tax Returns
- Claiming Child Benefit
- Submitting PAYE information if you are an employer
- Submitting CIS forms if you are a contractor
- Submitting VAT forms
- Submitting Corporation Tax forms
- Authorising an accountant to act on your behalf
- Submitting a range of HMRC standard forms
- Registering the commencement of your self-employment

How do I register with HMRC to use electronic services?

This is a two-stage process which is started on the HMRC website (www.gov.uk/log-in-register-hmrc-online-services/register). You will need to have your Unique Taxpayer Reference (UTR) and either your postcode or National Insurance number. On the HMRC website you will register and also sign up for at least one service, for example self-assessment. You will be given your 'User ID' during this process. When you have done this the government Gateway will post to you an Activation Code, which should be received within seven days. When you have both your User ID and the Activation Code you will be able to activate your account. However, the Activation Code is only valid for 28 days and if you do not activate your account during this time, you will have to go through the application process again.

E-mail scams

Unfortunately, there are a tremendous number of 'phishing' e-mails. These are e-mails which pretend to be from HMRC but which are in fact fraudulent. The purpose of these e-mails is to try to extract from the unwary, personal and financial details which the fraudsters can then use to steal money.

HMRC can only contact you by e-mail if you have provided your e-mail address to them. If you have opted for digital communications rather than paper communications, then as a private individual there are only two types of legitimate communication you will get from HMRC: a verification e-mail to check that your address works immediately after you have signed up to the electronic messaging service, and an e-mail telling you that there is a new message for you.

HMRC will never ask you to provide personal or financial information by e-mail.

HMRC will not say things like 'Only 3 days to reply' or 'urgent action required'.

Always look carefully at the e-mail address a message has come from. Look also for spelling mistakes, poor grammar and a broad greeting such as

'Dear customer'. Even if fraudsters have your e-mail address, they will rarely have your name. If you are in any doubt, report suspicious e-mails to HMRC at www.gov.uk/report-suspicious-emails-websites-phishing

Where does online banking fit into all this?

Online banking facilities are not connected to the HMRC electronic services. However, if you complete online VAT Returns you will also be required to make payment to HMRC electronically. Companies also have to pay their Corporation Tax online.

If you have online banking facilities then for speed and security we recommend using this method to make payments to HMRC. Always ensure that you provide the correct reference number with your payment.

Glossary

Additional rate tax	Income Tax at 45 per cent.
Agricultural property relief	This only relates to Inheritance Tax. Either a 50 per cent or 100 per cent reduction in the value of the agricultural property in the UK, Channel Isles or Isle of Man can be applied when listing the asset values for probate or valuing lifetime gifts.
AIM (Alternative Investment Market)	This is a Stock Exchange market whereby investors can deal in shares in smaller companies, most of which qualify for Inheritance Tax Business Property Relief. It was previously called the 'Unlisted Securities Market'.
Alimony	Money payable to a former spouse after divorce.
Annuity	An annual payment to an individual, usually resulting from a capital investment. The regular annual sums cease on death. Due to the payment mainly consisting of a return of capital, only a small part of the annuity usually bears tax at the basic rate.
AVC (Additional Voluntary Contribution)	These are additional contributions by an employee to his employer's approved pension scheme or to a separate pension provider of the employee's choosing (free-standing AVC).
Bare trust	A bare trust is one in which the beneficiary has an absolute entitlement to the income and the capital at any time.

Basic rate tax	Income Tax at 20 per cent.
Bed & breakfasting	Until the Spring Budget in 1998, it was common practice to take advantage of the annual tax-free Capital Gains Tax exemption by selling sufficient numbers of shares on one day (to realise a modest tax-free gain) only to buy them back the following day at more or less the same price. The 1998 Budget made bed & breakfasting ineffective for tax purposes, unless there is at least a 30-day gap between selling and repurchasing.
Beneficial loan	This is a loan by an employer to an employee at less than the official rate of interest.
Benefit in kind	Otherwise known as 'perks' received by a director or an employee which are nearly always taxed as employment income. From April 2015, any benefits costing under £50 do not need to be reported.
Blind Person's Allowance	An allowance of £2,290 which registered blind people can claim.
Bond	These are investments provided by insurance companies with apparently favourable tax treatment on both annual payment and final maturity. The annual payments and maturities are called 'chargeable events' by the taxman.
Capital allowance	These allowances are given to businesses for the purchase of capital assets (usually plant, equipment, machinery and motor vehicles), whereby the cost of the assets can be written down against tax over a period of years.
Capital Gains Tax	This is a tax on either the sale or gift of an asset, charging to tax the difference between the original cost and the value (sale proceeds) at disposal. If you make any capital gains as an individual, the first £11,100 gains are exempt from Capital Gains Tax.
Chargeable event	*See* Bond.

Class 1A National Insurance Contributions	These are special National Insurance contributions payable by employers on employees' benefits.
Corporation Tax	This is a tax levied on profits of limited companies.
Covenant	A payment under a deed of covenant in favour of a charity will normally benefit the charity, in that the basic rate tax paid by the individual can usually be reclaimed by the charity, thereby adding to its income, but deeds of covenant have largely been superseded by Gift Aid.
Director	A director is someone appointed by the shareholders to run a limited company. Sometimes people who are not called directors, nor formally appointed as such, by virtue of the activities they undertake in running the business, take on the same responsibilities and liabilities that a formal director attracts. Directors have certain extra responsibilities under tax law, particularly having to report on the taxable benefits they receive.
Discretionary trust	This is a type of trust whereby the trustees are given discretion as to the way in which they distribute income and capital to the various potential beneficiaries. In the case of other (non-discretionary) trusts the trustees are bound to pay the income over to the named beneficiaries.
Dividend	A dividend is a cash sum paid out of profits to shareholders of a company based on the number of shares they hold.
Domicile	The country or state which is your natural home. Professional advice should be sought over this, but someone who has a foreign domicile doesn't regard the UK as his real home. This can arise if the individual, or their father, was born outside the UK.
Earned income	This is the income of an individual which is derived from his physical, personal or mental labours. It also includes most pensions.

Emolument	This is a formal name given to salary, remuneration, bonuses and other income deriving from an employment of a director or employee.
Endowment	This usually is a form of life insurance involving payment by the insurer of a sum on a specified date, or on death.
Endowment mortgage	This is a mortgage linked to an endowment insurance policy with the mortgage being repaid from the sum insured. These have been largely superseded by repayment mortgages in recent years.
Enterprise Investment Scheme	This is a scheme under which individuals receive favourable Income Tax and Capital Gains Tax treatment when investing in qualifying unquoted trading companies.
Filing date	31 January, being the date following the end of the tax year by which your Self-Assessment Tax Return must have been submitted electronically to HM Revenue & Customs if you are to avoid an automatic £100 penalty. The filing date is 31 October if you send in a paper return.
Free-standing AVC	*See* AVC.
Fringe benefit	*See* Benefit in kind.
Gift Aid	Gift Aid covers individual single donations to charities from which, so long as enough basic rate tax has been paid by the donor, the charity is entitled to reclaim the tax. A form has to be filled in and handed to the charity. See Appendix 4.
Golden handshake	Term given to a lump sum payment made by an employer to an employee on the cessation of his employment. This can usually attract favourable tax treatment.
Gross income	Income from which no tax is deducted at source, even though tax may still have to be paid.
Higher-rate tax	Income Tax at 40 per cent.
Holdover relief	This is tax relief given to a donor, or other transferor of business assets, whereby the gain is not charged

to tax but deducted from the cost of the asset in the hands of the recipient.

Income Tax	This was the tax introduced in 1799 to pay for the Napoleonic Wars and is still with us today.
Indexation	Now available only to companies. This allowance provides for that element of a capital gain which is attributable to inflation.
Inheritance Tax	This is the tax payable on assets transferred on death and by way of lifetime gift, although estates (including transfers in the previous seven years) don't pay tax on the first £325,000.
Inheritance Tax exemption	It's possible to give away £3,000 each year (the annual exemption) with no Inheritance Tax implications. If you did not use the previous year's exemption, it's also possible to go back one year and include that as well, thereby doubling up the exemption to £6,000.
ISA (Individual Savings Account)	A tax-free savings account for individuals.
Lodger	See Rent-a-room relief.
Maintenance	A term for the payments made by one spouse to another after divorce.
Mortgage	A debt secured by a document (called a 'mortgage deed') which gives security to the lender for the debt. The mortgage deed must be returned at the time of settlement of the debt.
National Insurance	This is a levy applied to employment income and self-employment income, some of the contributions going towards the state pension on retirement and other contributory benefits.
Overlap relief	Where a self-employed person suffers tax more than once on a particular year's profits, a figure of overlap relief should be calculated so that, in due course, usually on the cessation of the business, this overpayment of tax may be taken into account.

PAYE (Pay As You Earn)	The compulsory system for employers to use whereby tax is deducted more or less evenly over the year resulting in the correct amount of tax being paid by the end of the tax year on an individual's earnings.
Potentially exempt transfer	A gift made by an individual that, so long as the donor lives for a further seven years, won't attract Inheritance Tax.
Private residence relief	This is the relief that exempts any gain on the sale of the home of an owner-occupier from Capital Gains Tax.
Rent-a-room relief	Special relief for individuals who let rooms to lodgers in their homes. Up to £7,500 per annum can be received in rent without any tax liability from 6 April 2016.
Rollover relief	This is a Capital Gains Tax relief that is available to an individual, partnership or company which disposes of one business asset and uses the proceeds to acquire a replacement business asset during a specified qualifying period.
Self-employed	Someone who is working in business on his own, preparing accounts and paying his own tax and National Insurance contributions. **Note:** It can be unclear if someone should be classified as employed or self-employed and in these cases professional advice should be sought.
Settlement	See Trust.
Share option	This is an option granted to directors or employees whereby they may buy shares in the company for which they work.
Stamp Duty	This is the duty payable on transfers of shares.
Stamp Duty Land Tax	This is the duty payable on transfers of property

Tax avoidance	Legally arranging your affairs in such a way as to reduce your tax liability.
Tax evasion	Illegally avoiding a tax liability – evade tax at your peril!
Term assurance	This is a cheap form of life assurance whereby, on the death of an individual within a certain specified time, a capital sum will be paid. This can be useful for providing for possible Inheritance Tax liabilities.
Trust (otherwise known as 'settlement')	Property is held in trust where the owner has passed it to trustees who hold it and manage it under the terms of the legal deed (called the 'trust deed') for the benefit of the beneficiaries. The trustees are the legal owners while the beneficiaries are the beneficial owners.
Unearned income	Income from investments and property as opposed to income earned.
Unincorporated business	Partnerships and sole traders are unincorporated businesses. Limited liability partnerships and limited companies are incorporated businesses.
Unit trust	An investment fund investing the combined contributions from individual investors and paying them dividends in proportion to their holding.
Venture Capital Trust	This is a type of investment trust for investing in unquoted trading companies with significant tax advantages for the investor.
Wasting asset	This is an asset that has an anticipated useful life of less than 50 years.
Wayleave	The land and property income deriving from sundry items such as telegraph and electricity poles.
Will	A legal document that shows how a deceased person wished his estate to be distributed, and who was to administer that estate.

Appendices

Appendix 1: 2015/2016 Tax rates and allowances at a glance

INCOME TAX

BAND	FROM	TO	RATE
Starting Rate for Savings*	£0	£5,000	Nil
Basic Rate	£0	£31,785	20%
Higher Rate	£31,786	£150,000	40%
Additional Rate	£150,001		45%

*If your non-savings income is above this limit then the 0% starting rate will not apply.
In addition to the ordinary rate for dividends there is the 32.5% higher rate and 37.5% additional rate.

CAPITAL GAINS TAX (for individuals)

First £11,000 exempt	18% for standard rate payers	28% for higher rate payers,	(10% if Entrepreneurs' Relief applies)

CORPORATION TAX

BAND	FROM	TO	RATE
Small Compnaies Rate	£1	£300,000	20%
Marginal Relief	£300,001	£1,500,000	20%
Main Rate	£1,500,001	-	20

INHERITANCE TAX (on death)

BAND	FROM	TO	RATE
Nil Rate Band	£0	£325,000	0%
Over Nil Rate Band	£325,001		40%

PERSONAL ALLOWANCES

Personal**	£10,600
Personal (aged 65-74)	£10,600
Personal (aged over 75)	£10,660
Married Couples (aged over 75)*#	£8,355

All three higher age allowances are only available for incomes up to £27,00 for 2015/16
* relief restricted to 10%
# husband or wife must be born before 6 April 1935
** The Personal Allowance reduces where income is above £100,000 - by £1 for every £2 of income over the £100,000 limit. This reduction applies irrespective of age.

NATIONAL INSURANCE

TYPE	EARNINGS PER WEEK	RATE
Class 1 (Employment)	*Employee (not contracted out)*	
	Up to £155	Nil
	£155 to £815	12%
	Over £815	2%
	Employer (not contracted out)	
	Up to £156	Nil
	Over £156	13.8%

Appendix 1: 2015/2016 Tax rates and allowances at a glance (cont.)

NATIONAL INSURANCE (CONTINUED)

TYPE	EARNINGS PER WEEK	RATE
Class 2 (Self-Employment)	(The old weekly stamp) No contributions due if profits below £5,965	£2.80
Class 4 (Self-Employment)	9% on profits between £8,060 and £42,385 2% on profits over £42,385	

STATE PENSION

	PER WEEK	PER YEAR
Single	£115.95	£6,029.40
Married	£185.45	£9,643.40
Age addition (over 80)	£0.25	£13.00

VAT

Threshold with effect from 1 April	£82,000
Rate	20%
Annual accounting threshold	£1,350,000
Cash accounting threshold	£1,350,000

STAMP DUTY LAND TAX ON RESIDENTIAL PROPERTY

From/to	0	£125,000	Nil*
From/to	£125,001	£250,000	2%
From/to	£250,001	£925,000	5%
From/to	£925,001	£1,500,000	10%
From/to	£1,500,001	-	12%
Acquisition of residential property over £500,000 by 'non-natural persons'			15%

TAXABLE CAR BENEFITS

Car Benefit	The scale charge is based on CO_2 emissions. The annual charge ranges from 5% for eco-friendly cars to 35% for gas guzzlers. There is no adjustment for the age of car, nor for business mileage. Alternative rates apply to cars registered before 01.01.1998. Diesels attract a 3% surcharge, but not over 35%. Electric cars and vans have 0% benefit charge.	
Fuel Benefit	As with Car Benefit, the taxable charge is based on CO_2 emissions. The charge is based on a sum of £22,100 for all cars, not on the price of the car.	
Van Benefit	Any age of vehicle	
	Van Scale Charge	£3,150
	Fuel Scale Charge for Vans	£594

CAR MILEAGE ALLOWANCE

ALL ENGINE SIZES	
Up to 10,000 miles pa	45p
Over 10,000 miles pa	25p

Appendix 2: 2016/2017 Tax rates and allowances at a glance

INCOME TAX

BAND	FROM	TO	RATE
Starting Rate for Savings*	£0	£5,000	Nil
Basic Rate	£0	£32,000	20%
Higher Rate	£32,001	£150,000	40%
Additional Rate	£150,001		45%

*If your non-savings income is above this limit then the 10% starting rate will not apply.

PROPERTY CAPITAL GAINS TAX (for individuals)

First £11,000 exempt	18% for standard rate payers	28% for higher rate payers,	(10% if Entrepreneurs' Relief applies)

NON-PROPERTY CAPITAL GAINS TAX (for individuals)

First £11,000 exempt	10% for standard rate payers	20% for higher rate payers	(10% if Entrepreneurs' Relief applies)

CORPORATION TAX

Small Companies Rate and Main Rate	20%

DIVIDEND TAXATION

Dividend Allowance	£5,000
Liability on dividends in excess of £5,000 within basic tax rate band	7.5%
Liability on dividends in excess of £5,000 within higher tax rate band	32.5%
Liability on dividends in excess of £5,000 within additional tax rate band	38.1%

PERSONAL SAVINGS ALLOWANCE

Basic rate taxpayers	£1,000
Higher rate tax payers	£500
Additional rate tax payers	£0

INHERITANCE TAX (on death)

BAND	FROM	TO	RATE
Nil Rate Band	£0	£325,000	0%
Over Nil Rate Band	£325,001		40%

PERSONAL ALLOWANCES

Personal*	£11,000
Married Couples (aged over 75)#	£8,165

Married Couples Allowances are only available for incomes up to £27,700 for 2016/17. This allowance is then reduced by £1 for every £2 of income over £27,700, until the allowance is reduced to the minimum level of £3,220.

* the Personal Allowance reduces where income is above £100,000 - by £1 for every £2 of income over the £100,000 limit. This reduction applies irrespective of age.

relief restricted to 10% and husband or wife must be born before 6 April 1935.

Appendix 2: 2016/2017 Tax rates and allowances at a glance (cont.)

NATIONAL INSURANCE

TYPE	EARNINGS PER WEEK	RATE
Class 1 (Employment)	*Employee (not contracted out)*	
	Up to £155	Nil
	£155 to £827	12%
	Over £827	2%
	Employer (not contracted out)	
	Up to £156	Nil
	Over £156	13.8%
Class 2 (Self-employment)	(The old weekly stamp) No contributions due if profits below £5,965	£2.80
Class 4 (Self-employment)	9% on profits between £8,060 and £43,000 2% on profits over £43,000	

STATE PENSION

	PER WEEK	PER YEAR
Single	£119.30	£6,203.60
Married	£190.80	£9,921.60
Age addition (over 80)	£0.25	£13.00
New state pension	£155.65	£8,093.80

VAT

Threshold with effect from 1 April	£83,000
Rate	20%
Annual accounting threshold	£1,350,000
Cash accounting threshold	£1,350,000

STAMP DUTY LAND TAX ON RESIDENTIAL PROPERTY

			RATE	2ND PROPERTY RATE
From/to	0	£125,000	Nil*	3%
From/to	£125,001	£250,000	2%	5%
From/to	£250,001	£925,000	5%	8%
From/to	£925,001	£1,500,000	10%	13%
From/to	£1,500,001		12%	15%
Acquisition of residential property over £500,000 by 'non-natural persons'			15%	

TAXABLE CAR BENEFITS

Car Benefit	The scale charge is based on CO_2 emissions. The annual charge ranges from 5% for eco-friendly cars to 37% for gas guzzlers. There is no adjustment for the age of car, nor for business mileage. Alternative rates apply to cars registered before 01.01.1998. Diesels attract a 3% surcharge, but not over 35%. Electric cars and vans have 0% benefit charge.
Fuel Benefit	As with Car Benefit, the taxable charge is based on CO_2 emissions. The charge is based on a sum of £22,200 for all cars, not on the price of the car.
Van Benefit	Any age of vehicle
	Van Scale Charge — £3,170
	Fuel Scale Charge for Vans — £598

CAR MILEAGE ALLOWANCE

ALL ENGINE SIZES	
Up to 10,000 miles pa	45p
Over 10,000 miles pa	25p

Appendix 3: Checklist of what to keep for your Tax Return

For Income Tax

If you receive	Keep your
☐ **Salary/wages**	Payslips (supplied by your employer) P60 (annual statement of earnings from your employer) Notice of coding (issued by HM Revenue & Customs)
☐ **Benefits in kind** (e.g. company car, medical insurance)	P11D (annual statement of benefits) and expense payments from your employer
☐ **State benefits** (e.g. Jobseeker's Allowance, Carer's Allowance)	Statements of payments to you by the Department for Work and Pensions (DWP)
☐ **Pensions** State pension, other pensions	Statement of pension payments by the Department for Work and Pensions (DWP) or pension funds, etc.
☐ **Share options** (offered by some employers)	Share option documents from your employer
☐ **Other earnings** Tips, commissions and other earnings	Relevant vouchers
☐ **Expenses not reimbursed** by your employer	Expense receipts
☐ **Self-employment and partnerships** Income from self-employment	Self-employed or partnership accounts
☐ **Savings and deposit accounts** Banks Building societies National Savings	Bank interest certificates Building society interest certificates National Savings interest details

Appendix 3: Checklist of what to keep for your Tax Return (continued)

☐ **Shareholdings**
Dividends — Dividend vouchers
Unit trusts — Unit trust vouchers

☐ **Other sources**
Annuities — Annuity vouchers
Other — Relevant vouchers

☐ **Land and property**
Furnished holiday accommodation — Copy invoices or receipts for rental
Furnished and unfurnished lettings — income, etc.
(including rent-a-room) — Receipts or supporting evidence of
Wayleaves (e.g. electricity poles) — expenditure

If you receive income from	Keep your
☐ **Overseas**	Foreign income documents (e.g. dividends, pensions and interest) Foreign property income
☐ **Trusts and settlements**	Trust tax vouchers (R185), issued by trustees or executors
☐ **Other sources** such as:	
Alimony	Alimony details
Royalties	Royalty income and expenses
Bonds, etc.	Chargeable event certificates, etc.

Deductions to claim against Income Tax

☐ **Interest** — Loan interest statements

☐ **Venture Capital Trust shares** — Venture Capital Trust certificates

☐ **Enterprise Investment Scheme subscriptions** — Enterprise Investment Scheme certificates

☐ **Seed Enterprise Investment Scheme** — Seed Enterprise Investment Scheme certificates

Appendix 3: Checklist of what to keep for your Tax Return (continued)

☐	**Charitable covenants**	Deeds of covenant
☐	**Gift Aid**	Gift Aid details
☐	**Death benefits to trade union or friendly society**	Death benefit papers
☐	Or if you are **registered blind**	Relevant papers

For Capital Gains Tax

☐	**Shares**	Contract notes from your stockbroker
☐	**Land and property**	Estate agent's particulars Completion statements (from solicitors)
☐	**Paintings or other works of art**	Auction advice slips Sales catalogues
☐	**Businesses** or parts of them	Completion statements from professional advisers

Appendix 4: A template to help you prepare your figures for the self-employed part of the Tax Return

Your name _____ Accounting year end _____

Self-employment and Partnerships

Sales income   A

less   **Costs of sales,** e.g. raw materials and stocks

Construction industry subcontractors' costs

Other direct costs, e.g. packing and despatch

Total cost of sales   B

Gross profit or loss A – B   C

Other income   D

Expenditure

Employee costs
Salaries, wages, bonuses, employer's NIC, pension contributions,
casual wages, canteen costs, recruitment agency fees,
subcontractors (unless shown above) and other wages costs

Premises costs
Rent, ground rent, rates, water, refuse, light and heat, property
insurance, security and use of home

Repairs
Repair of property, replacements, renewals, maintenance

General administrative expenses
Telephone, fax, mobile telephone, stationery, photocopying, printing,
postage, courier and computer costs, subscriptions, insurance

Motoring expenses
Fuel, servicing, licence, repairs, motor insurance, hire and
leasing, car parking, RAC/AA membership

Travel and subsistence
Rail, air, bus, etc., travel, taxis, subsistence and hotel costs

Entertainment
Staff entertaining (e.g. Christmas party), customer gifts up to £50
per person advertising your business

Advertising and promotion
Advertising, promotion, mailshots, free samples, brochures,
newsletters, trade shows, etc.

Legal and professional costs
Accountancy, legal, architects, surveyors, stocktakers' fees,
indemnity insurance

Bad debts (if already included in A above)

Interest
on bank loans, overdraft and other loans

Other finance charges
Bank charges, HP interest, credit card charges, leasing not
already included

Depreciation and profits/losses on sale (please ask for advice)

Other items – please describe

Grand total of expenses   E

Net profit (or loss) C + D – E

Appendix 5: Gift Aid declaration

giftaid it

Gift Aid declaration –for a single donation

Name of charity or Community Amateur Sports Club

Please treat the enclosed gift of £ ------------------------- as a Gift Aid donation.

I confirm I have paid or will pay an amount of Income Tax and/or Capital Gains Tax for the current tax year (6 April to 5 April) that is at least equal to the amount of tax that all the charities and Community Amateur Sports Clubs (CASCs) that I donate to will reclaim on my gifts for the current tax year. I understand that other taxes such as VAT and Council Tax do not qualify. I understand the charity will reclaim 25p of tax on every £1 that I have given.

Donor's details

Title ------------ First name or initial(s) ---

Surname --

Full Home address ---

Postcode ----------------------------------

Date ---

Signature ---

Please notify the charity or CASC if you:

- *Want to cancel this declaration*
- *Change your name or home address*
- *No longer pay sufficient tax on your income and/or capital gains.*

If you pay Income Tax at the higher or additional rate and want to receive the additional tax relief due to you, you must include all your Gift Aid donations on your Self Assessment tax return or ask HM Revenue and Customs to adjust your tax code.

Source: HMRC

Appendix 6: A template to help you prepare your figures for the land and property income part of the Tax Return

Your name _____

Land and Property Income (year to 5 April   )

Income Received from   Rents received
£

_____

_____

_____

Total income   £

Tax already deducted from property income   £

£   £

Expenditure

Premises	Rents	_____
	Rates	_____
	Property insurance	_____
	Light and heat	_____
	Cleaning	_____
	Security	_____
	Subtotal	

Repairs and maintenance	Repairs and renewals	_____
	Redecorating	_____
	Small tools	_____
	Subtotal	

Finance charges and interest on loan to buy rented property

Legal and professional	Legal	_____
	Accountancy	_____
	Debt collection	_____
	Other insurances	_____
	Subscriptions	_____
	Architects' fees	_____
	Subtotal	

Services provided	Wages	_____
	Telephone	_____
	TV	_____
	Garden	_____
	Roads	_____
	Subtotal	

Other costs	Advertising	_____
	Agents' fees	_____
	Office costs	_____
	Travel	_____
	Subtotal	

Total expenditure   £

Appendix 7: A rough guide to Capital Gains Tax and Inheritance Tax
(see Notes on the following page)

The effect of a of following items on	Gift CGT	Gift IHT	Sale CGT	Sale IHT	Death CGT	Death IHT
Own residence	None	Normally none, but donee must retain assets for seven years and donor must survive seven years.	None	None	None	Taxable - see note 3
Business assets:						
Land used in business	Taxable		Taxable	None	None	There should be 100% relief.
Goodwill	Taxable		Taxable	None	None	
Furnished lettings business	Taxable		Taxable	None	None	
Partnerships	Taxable		Taxable	None	None	
Other assets	Taxable		Taxable	None	None	
Milk, etc. quotas	Taxable		Taxable	None	None	See note 4
Woodlands	Not taxable†		Not taxable◊	None	None	
Shares in small business	Taxable		Taxable	None	None	
Let property subject to:						
Gladstone vs. Bowers tenancies	Taxable - see note 1	Tapering relief* after three years	Taxable - see note 1	None	None	Should be 100% relief
Residential tenancies	Taxable - see note 2		Taxable - see note 2	None	None	Taxable - see note 3
Farm business tenancies	Taxable - see note 1		Taxable - see note 1	None	None	Should be 100% relief
Other business tenancies	Taxable - see note 1		Taxable - see note 1	None	None	Should be 50% relief
Heritage properties	Normally taxable – see note 5		Normally taxable	None	None	Not taxable
Works of art	Taxable - see note 2		Taxable - see note 2	None	None	Taxable - see note 3
Loans to a business	Should be no CGT		Should be no CGT	None	None	Taxable - see note 3
Stock Exchange investments	Taxable - see note 2		Taxable - see note 2	None	None	Taxable - see note 3
Lloyds investments	Taxable - see note 1		Taxable - see note 1	None	None	Should be 100% relief
Trusts (interest in possession)	- Not applicable	N/A	Not applicable	N/A	None	Taxable - see note 3

*Tapering relief tax charge: Death within 3 years - 100%; death within 3-4 years - 80%; death within 4-5 years - 60%; death within 5-6 years - 40%; death within 6-7 years - 20%; death after 7 years - 0%

†Standing or felled trees do not attract CGT but the land itself is subject to it

This is only a rough guide; professional advice MUST be sought before taking action

Appendix 7: A rough guide to Capital Gains Tax and Inheritance Tax (cont.)

Notes to Appendix 6

Note 1

Disposals of business assets are subject to a number of Capital Gains Tax reliefs but seek professional advice, because this is only a brief summary:

EIS deferral relief – an investment in shares in an unquoted trading company defers the gain. The acquisition cost is reduced by the gain.

Rollover relief – where the disposal of business assets leads to replacement business assets being acquired, the gain on disposal is not charged to tax but the cost of the new assets is reduced by the gain.

Capital Gains Tax annual exemption – £11,100.

Note 2

The following are ways in which Capital Gains Tax may be reduced or legally avoided:

EIS deferral relief – an investment in shares in an unquoted trading company defers the gain. The acquisition cost is reduced by the gain.

Capital Gains Tax annual exemption – £11,100.

Business losses – trading losses may be set against capital gains of that year or of the previous year, but only if they have first been set against the individual's general income for that year.

Enterprise Investment Schemes (EIS) – an annual investment of up to £1,000,000 secures Income Tax relief of 30 per cent. Capital Gains Tax deferral relief will be available on EIS.

Seed Enterprise Investment Scheme (SEIS) – an annual investment of up to £100,000; secures Income Tax relief of 50 per cent. Capital Gains Tax relief also available.

Venture Capital Trust (VCT) – an annual investment of up to £200,000 secures Income Tax relief of 30 per cent.

Note 3

Assets passing on death normally attract Inheritance Tax at 40 per cent, but the first £325,000 is tax free. Also, transfers to the spouse of the deceased are normally exempt.

Note 4

Property used in a business which is owned by a partner or property used in a business which is controlled by the shareholder attracts only 50 per cent relief. The property must have been used and owned for two years. Shares giving control in an agricultural company attract 100 per cent relief. Shares in a private trading company attract 100 per cent relief. Controlling shareholdings in quoted companies attract 50 per cent relief.

Note 5

There may be holdover relief available.

> **This is only a rough guide; professional advice MUST be sought before taking action**

Appendix 8: A template to help you work out your Inheritance Tax bill and plan to make a Will

I own	Estimated value	At my death I would like to leave this to:
House		
Valuables		
Shares		
Cash		
Other land and property		
Trust		
Business assets		
The residue of my estate		
Legacies I would like to give		Details:
Substantial gifts I have made in the last seven years		Gifted to:
Less Sums I owe	( )	How will these be repaid on death?
Total estate		
Less tax-free band	**(£325,000)**	
Less unused tax-free band of deceased spouse/civil partner (only available when the second death is after 8 October 2007)	**(x)**	
Total net		
Tax due @ 40%		

Appendix 9: Personal fact sheet

If you were to die today, how would your family and executors find your papers, etc. and sort everything out? This personal fact sheet is a way of helping you and your survivors.

You might like to fill this in, to keep a copy yourself and place a copy with your Will.

A **Full name** (including title and decorations)

Date of birth _____ Place of birth _____

Tax reference no. _____

State pension no. _____

National Insurance no. _____

Others _____

_____

_____

_____

This personal fact sheet prepared (date) _____

B **My Will**

Made on _____

Reviewed on _____

Is kept at _____

_____

_____

_____

My executors are _____ Tel no. _____

_____ Tel no. _____

_____ Tel no. _____

_____ Tel no. _____

Appendix 9: Personal fact sheet (cont.)

C **Substantial gifts made before death**

Date of gift   Date   Value

_____

_____

D **Location of other key documents**

Funeral wishes
_____

Keys to safe
_____

Birth certificate
_____

Marriage certificate
_____

Insurance policies
_____

Pension policies
_____

Property and mortgage deeds
_____

Bank statements
_____

Building society passbooks
_____

Medical card
_____

Car documents
_____

Share certificates
_____

Other investment certificates
_____

Where to find brief biographical details for any obituary
(suggest who else might be able to write this)

_____

_____

Trust deeds
_____

Leases of rented property
_____

Partnership deed (copy)
_____

Appendix 9: Personal fact sheet (cont.)

E   People to contact

Accountant

Solicitor

Stockbroker

Insurance broker

Bankers

Pension payer

Tax Office

Employer

Doctor

Trustees

Life assurance

Any other key adviser

F   My business affairs

Details

Directorships

Partnerships

G   My insurance policies

On my death the following policies mature   Location

Appendix 9: Personal fact sheet (cont.)

H **Employment history**

From   To   Employer   Address

I **My pension arrangements**

Pensions payable by

Tel no.

Annuities I receive

J **Other assets**

Details of other assets not already listed

K **Liabilities**

Debts I owe   Loans

Overdrafts

HP debts

Mortgages

Guarantees I have made to

on behalf of   for £

L **Clubs and organisations I belong to**

M **Who else has a copy of this form?**

Appendix 10: Notable tax dates

Date	Significance of Date	Employers	Individual Tax Payers	Partners and Sole Traders
19/4/2016	Deadline for settling 2014/15 PAYE and National Insurance contributions – interest will be charged from this date on overdue balances	✓		
	Deadline for Payroll Year-End Submission. Month 12 FPS electronic report must be shown as the final one for the year	✓		
31/5/2016	Deadline date for getting P60 forms to employees	✓		
6/7/2016	Deadline date for sending P11D forms to employees	✓		
	Deadline date for sending P11D forms and P11D(b) Return of Class 1A National Insurance contributions due to HMRC	✓		
19/7/2016	Payment of Class 1A National Insurance contributions to HMRC	✓	✓	✓
31/7/2016	Second instalments of Income Tax and Class 4 National Insurance re 2015/16 are due		✓	✓
	Another £100 fine for late submission of 2014/15 Tax Return		✓	✓
3/8/2016	A further five per cent surcharge where tax due for 2014/15 still outstanding		✓	✓
31/10/2016	Deadline for submission of 2015/16 paper Tax Return and for tax calculation by HMRC – for penalty, see next section		✓	✓
31/1/2017	Deadline for electronic submission of 2015/16 Tax Return. Late filers will be charged a £100 fine (and in the case of a late partnership return each partner will be fined £100) and interest on overdue tax		✓	✓
	Balance of tax due for 2015/16		✓	✓
	First payment on account for 2016/17 tax year		✓	✓
3/3/2017	A five per cent surcharge where tax due for 2015/16 still outstanding		✓	✓
5/4/2017	End of 2016/17 tax year	✓	✓	✓

Appendix 10: Notable tax dates (cont.)

Date	Significance of Date	Employers	Individual Tax Payers	Partners and Sole Traders
19/4/2017	Deadline for settling 2016/17 PAYE and National Insurance contributions – interest will be charged from this date on overdue balances	✓		
	Deadline for Payroll Year-End Submission. Month 12 FPS electronic report must be shown as the final one for the year	✓		
31/5/2017	Deadline date for getting P60 forms to employees	✓		
6/7/2017	Deadline date for sending P11D forms to employees	✓		
	Deadline date for sending P11D forms and P11D(F) Return of Class 1A National Insurance contributions due to HMRC	✓		
19/7/2017	Payment of Class 1A National Insurance contributions to HMRC	✓	✓	✓
31/7/2017	Second instalments of Income Tax and Class 4 National Insurance re 2016/17 are due		✓	✓
	Another £100 fine for late submission of 2015/16 Tax Return.			
3/8/2017	A further five per cent surcharge where tax due for 2015/16 still outstanding		✓	✓
31/10/2017	Deadline for submission of 2016/17 paper Tax Return and for tax calculation by HMRC – for penalty, see next section		✓	✓
31/1/2018	Deadline for electronic submission of 2016/17 Tax Return. Late filers will be charged a £100 fine (and in the case of a late partnership return each partner will be fined £100) and interest on overdue tax		✓	✓
	Balance of tax due for 2016/17		✓	✓
	First payment on account for 2017/18 tax year		✓	✓
3/3/2018	A five per cent surcharge where tax due for 2016/17 still outstanding		✓	✓

Appendix 11: Tax reliefs available for investment in unquoted companies

Tax reliefs available for investment in unquoted companies

	Income Tax Relief on Amount Invested	Capital Gains Tax Deferral	Tax-Free Income	Tax-Free Gains	Income Tax Relief on Losses	Losses Offsettable against Capital Gains
Purchasing shares directly	No	No	No	No	Yes	Yes
Enterprise Investment Scheme	Yes	Yes	No	Yes	Yes	Yes
Venture Capital Trusts	Yes	No	Yes	Yes	No	No
Seed EIS	Yes	50%	Yes	Yes	Yes	Yes

Appendix 12: VAT fuel scale charges for three-month periods

CO$_2$ band	VAT Fuel Scale Charge, 3-month period £	VAT on 3-month charge £	VAT exclusive 3-month charge £
120 or less	116.00	19.30	96.67
125	175.00	29.17	145.83
130	186.00	31.00	155.00
135	197.00	32.83	164.17
140	209.00	34.83	174.17
145	221.00	36.83	184.17
150	233.00	38.83	194.17
155	245.00	40.83	204.17
160	256.00	42.67	213.33
165	268.00	44.67	223.33
170	279.00	46.50	232.50
175	291.00	48.50	242.50
180	303.00	50.50	252.50
185	314.00	52.33	261.67
190	326.00	54.33	271.67
195	338.00	56.33	281.67
200	350.00	58.33	291.67
205	362.00	60.33	301.67
210	373.00	62.17	310.83
215	384.00	64.00	320.00
220	396.00	66.00	330.00
225 or more	408.00	68.00	340.00

Where the CO$_2$ emission figure is not a multiple of 5, the figure is rounded down to the next multiple of 5 to determine the level of the charge. For a bi-fuel vehicle which has two CO$_2$ emissions figures, the lower of the two figures should be used. For cars which are too old to have a CO$_2$ emissions figure, you should identify the CO$_2$ band based on engine size, as follows:

If its cylinder capacity is 1,400cc or less, use CO$_2$ band 140.

If its cylinder capacity exceeds 1,400cc but does not exceed 2,000cc, use CO$_2$ band 175.

If its cylinder capacity exceeds 2,000cc, use CO$_2$ band 225 or above.

Before deciding to reclaim the VAT on your fuel, you should look at the amount you will be reclaiming and what the VAT fuel scale charge is, to see whether it is worth it.

Index

This index covers chapters, but not appendices or Glossary.
Terms refer to taxation.

Notes

Notes

Notes